summer

summer

a user's guide

suzanne brown

artisan » new york

Grateful acknowledgment is made for permission to reprint the following:

Lyrics from "Surf City," words and music by Brian Wilson and Jan Berry.
Copyright © 1963 (renewed 1991) by Screen Gems–EMI Music, Inc.
All rights reserved. International copyright secured. Used by permission.

Ice cream sandwich recipe from *The Ultimate Ice Cream Book* by Bruce Weinstein.
Copyright © 1999 by Bruce Weinstein. Reprinted by permission of
HarperCollinsPublishers.

Published by Artisan
A Division of Workman Publishing Company, Inc.
225 Varick Street
New York, NY 10014-4381
www.artisanbooks.com

Library of Congress Cataloging-in-Publication Data

Brown, Suzanne
Summer / Suzanne Brown.
p. cm.
ISBN-13: 978-1-57965-316-3
ISBN-10: 1-57965-316-2
1. Cookery 2. Handicraft 3. Amusement I. Title.
TX714.B794 2007
641.5—dc22   2006049903

Design by Jan Derevjanik

Printed in China
First printing, April 2007

10 9 8 7 6 5 4 3 2 1

Me in my first bikini

To my parents, Barbara and John, for a lifetime of love and support. Thank you for believing in me.

To my brothers, John and Michael, for countless summer memories. What a shame that I am the only one who remembers the chocolate-covered bananas from Bill's Deli—they were truly delicious.

And especially to my husband, Jerry, without whom this book wouldn't have been possible. It was your love of summer that inspired me. Thank you for being with me every step of the way. You are the reason I wake up each morning.

Jerry's favorite key lime pie

My husband loves key lime pie so much that I promised in my wedding vows that I would make it for him at least three times a year. This is for him.

- One 14-ounce can sweetened condensed milk
- 3 egg yolks
- ½ cup key lime juice
- 1 tablespoon finely grated lime peel
- One 9-inch prebaked graham cracker pie shell (you can make your own or purchase one)
- Whipped cream for garnish (optional)
- Mint leaves for garnish (optional)

Preheat the oven to 350°F.

In a mixing bowl, combine the milk, egg yolks, lime juice, and lime peel and blend until smooth. Pour the mixture into the pie shell and back in the preheated oven for 15 minutes.

Remove from the oven and allow the pie to stand for approximately 10 minutes, then refrigerate.

Enjoy plain or garnish with a dollop of whipped cream, a sprig of mint, or both.

》 serves 6–8

contents

games, indoors and out

the summer table

introduction

I'm madly in love with summer and the feelings it evokes—the carefree spirit of freedom and adventure that fall, winter, and spring simply don't provide. Summer entices us to lose our inhibitions, to have fun, to be curious, and to seek adventure. We are joyous upon its arrival in June and bittersweet as it fades into September. Summer is fabulous, but fleeting.

I've had the good fortune to spend many summers in places other than my "real" home. As a child, my family spent the season in an old beach bungalow on the Jersey shore. Looking back, it seems to me that we spent every waking moment outdoors—at the beach during the day, kite flying after dinner, at miniature golf or on the boardwalk in the evening. In the early mornings, my father—whom I've never seen happier than when he has a fishing pole or crab net in his hands—would bring us to the pier, where we'd drop the crab nets into inky waters, ever impatient to pull them up and see what we caught. Hours later, we'd return home with buckets of blue crabs, which my mother would magically turn into a delicious crab salad. My mom loves to tell the Annie Hall–esque story of the wily crab that went on the lam across our kitchen floor, eventually finding safe refuge behind the stove. Alas, his freedom didn't last for long; after much bedlam, my parents somehow managed to extract him from his hideaway and get him into the steamer pot.

As a young woman, I frequently spent summer weekends with family friends in their fabulous home nestled in the woods of Martha's Vineyard. We'd wake up at sunrise and cook pancakes and sausages outside on the grill, then head off to the beach, where we'd spend hours combing the sand for sharks' teeth, shells, and beach glass. On special evenings, we'd drive their jalopy—a 1969 Dodge Dart—to Menemsha, where we'd crack open freshly cooked lobsters and watch the sun set. What wonderful, effortless days those were.

My passion for the outdoors led me to Maine, where I summered for many years on a quiet cove in ruggedly beautiful Bar Harbor. Down East I braved frigid waters, hiked endless wooded paths, and biked along meandering carriage trails shaded by an awning of pines. Exhausted from whatever the day's activities were, I'd reward myself with a hearty lobster roll or a bucket of steamers, then drift off to sleep to the rhythmic sound of the ocean.

Lest you think I'm only content breathing in salt air, rest assured that I equally adore the clean, pure scent of fresh water. My love affair with lakes began at a friend's cabin in the Adirondacks. A natural gathering spot on long weekends, we'd paddle canoes, water-ski behind a balky old powerboat, drift aimlessly on a pontoon, or lounge on fat tire tubes. After years spent on the ocean, the lakefront lifestyle was a delightful new experience of slithering fish, slippery green rocks, and no undercurrents. As quaint as it might seem, at day's end we'd all gather around a campfire to roast marshmallows, talk, and laugh deep into the night, heading to bed in the wee hours, smelling of smoke.

Of course, being a New Yorker, I can't dismiss my summers in the city; just because I love the outdoors doesn't mean I don't equally love watching the sun set over the Hudson from a Manhattan terrace while sipping a glass of good champagne. My friends Christophe and Léa throw the most wonderful parties on the roof of their downtown apartment building. There's always a fashionable and cosmopolitan crowd, and most times I forget the hour and have to race like Cinderella to Grand Central to catch the last train back home.

I'm married now, and my husband and I spend our summers along the perpetually sunny coast of South Carolina. Everything moves at a slower pace there, and we're no exception. As a rule, we do nothing more ambitious than shell-seeking, biking along the beach, sea kayaking, and making an occasional stop at a nearby beach bar for a refreshing frozen cocktail. It was on one of these vacations, on a stretch of endless white sand on Hilton Head Island, that I began thinking deeply about all the things I love about summer. I realized that if sheer pleasure makes for expertise, then few are more qualified than I am to write on the essence and the spirit of the season.

On these pages, you'll find ideas for living life to the fullest in the summer months. I've included all of the crafts, recipes, music, and games that I personally look forward to each year—plus I've thrown in practical how-to's and a hefty dose of nostalgia to conjure up days past. It's my hope that this book will inspire all of you to embrace the carefree warm-weather lifestyle wherever you might be and whatever the season—after all, summer is not just a time of year, but a state of mind.

50 fun things to do this summer

1. Build a gigantic sand castle
2. Cook Sunday breakfast on the grill
3. Spend an afternoon floating in a tire tube
4. Learn to play croquet
5. Run through a sprinkler
6. Start an herb garden
7. Go bodysurfing
8. Send a message in a bottle
9. Rent a bicycle built for two
10. Learn how to identify stars
11. Make a summer shadow box
12. Try to find sharks' teeth on the beach
13. Tie-dye T-shirts
14. Press flowers
15. Make a necklace out of dandelions
16. Serve root-beer floats for dessert
17. Hold a bocce tournament
18. Install an outdoor shower
19. Ride a roller coaster
20. Tell ghost stories around a campfire
21. Hang a tire swing in the backyard
22. Have an egg-throwing contest
23. Go skinny-dipping
24. Organize a clambake
25. Grow sunflowers
26. Put up a clothesline
27. Hang a hummingbird feeder
28. Take surfing lessons
29. Fill your house with fresh-cut daisies
30. Make seashell candles
31. Take underwater portraits
32. Go clamming
33. Make a rope swing
34. Hang a hammock between shady trees

35 Hold a film festival on a rainy weekend

36 Bake zucchini bread for neighbors and friends

37 Make seashell wind chimes

38 Eat a lobster roll

39 Keep a summer diary

40 Grow watermelon

41 Make a pitcher of sun tea

42 Buy (and wear) madras plaid shorts

43 Ride your bike on the beach at low tide

44 Make grilled pizza

45 Squeeze fresh lemonade

46 Rent a kayak

47 Refuse to wear anything on your
   feet except flip-flops

48 Hang a butterfly feeder

49 Make s'mores

50 Spike a watermelon with vodka

the summer house and garden

In what should be a blissful, stress-free season, challenges inevitably arise that may require a refresher course—things like lighting charcoal, getting rid of pesky bugs, and removing splinters. For years I clipped helpful articles from magazines and newspapers, thinking they would eventually come in handy; but they were scattered everywhere, and when I needed a particular one, it was impossible to find. Finally, I got wise and bought a bunch of inexpensive binders; now all my articles are nicely organized by topic and easy to get my hands on. Stain on a white linen blouse—the solution is there. What to whip up when unexpected guests arrive? I have that covered too.

For those of you who don't have your own handy "How To" binder at your summer house, here's a chapter filled with helpful tips and directions that will allow you to spend less time on chores, more time on relaxing. Whether you stay at home for the summer, spend time at your weekend getaway, or rent a country house for two weekends or more, I hope this section makes the warmer months easier and more pleasurable.

HOW TO make your summer rental shine

You've waited all year for your summer vacation, and when you finally get there, your dream home is less than dreamy. Don't let a disappointing rental ruin your fun—w--home. Since it's not your place, you certainly can't start painting walls and buying new furniture, but you can head to stores like Target, Wal-Mart, or Kmart for stylish, inexpensive accessories that will cheer the place up without costing you a fortune.

Consider investing in

» **Area rugs.** You'll be amazed at what a fresh rug will do for a room.

» **Throw pillows.** Scatter them on chairs, sofas, beds, the floor.

» **Bright fabrics.** They could be sheets, blankets, remnants. Hem or not and spread one over a dingy sofa, use another as a tablecloth, bring another to the beach as a blanket, fashion as a window curtain or valence. (If you're unsure of how much fabric to buy, I've provided some common measurements in the box on page 25.)

» **Lighting.** Grab a few inexpensive lamps or paper lanterns to add a warm glow to the house.

» **A new shower curtain, soft towels, and scented soaps** will add luxury to the bathroom.

» **Fun plastic drinking glasses.** Break-free for the patio.

» **Indoor plants.** They really do make a house feel more like a home.

» **A wind sock or outdoor flag.** A nice way to welcome guests.

There are many other things you can do to freshen up a summer rental.

THROUGHOUT THE HOUSE

» Open all the windows and let the house air out for a few hours.

» A softly scented room spray will cover up any odd smells that may be lingering. Furniture, rugs, and curtains can trap odors, so spray them with Febreze.

» Place a few scented candles on a large platter with seashells, beach glass, or any other treasures you find outdoors.

» Place bunches of colorful flowers in each room. If there are no vases handy, use jelly jars or tall glasses. Cut stems short for sweet bouquets.

IN THE BEDROOMS

» Sprinkle some baby powder and baking soda on musty mattresses to remove odors.

» Bring your own pillows and sheets, or treat yourself to new ones. I can't sleep without my down pillow and my soft jersey pillowcase, so they come with me wherever I travel. When you're in a strange bed, it's nice to have your own soft linens to help you feel comfortable.

IN THE KITCHEN

» Get rid of stale kitchen odors by mixing ¼ cup of vinegar and 1 quart of water in a large saucepan and bringing to a boil on the stove. Five to ten minutes of steam releases odor-neutralizing vinegar particles into the air.

» Grind some lemon and orange peels in the garbage disposal to clear up unpleasant odors.

» Cook! Even if you hate being in the kitchen on vacation, the scent of coffee brewing and slices of raisin bread toasting can make a huge difference.

IN GENERAL

» If it's *that* bad, grab a phone book and hire a cleaning person to do the work for you.

» Pop your favorite album in the CD player to cheer yourself up.

» Sometimes it's good to make light of a bad situation. Buy some inexpensive disposable cameras and take wacky pictures of your family and friends, so you can always look back on your "summerhouse from hell" and laugh!

» When all else fails, make a batch of fresh mango margaritas to lift your spirits. With kids, make a batch of smoothies (page 217) or blow bubbles (page 192) with them while you sip your margarita (page 132).

Working with Fabric

SHEET SIZE
For bedding, as beach blankets, or to drape over furniture.

Twin	66" x 96"
Double	81" x 96"
Queen	90" x 102"
Standard king	108" x 102"
California king	102" x 110"

TABLECLOTHS

Square	52" x 52" for tables that measure 28" x 28" to 40" x 40". These tables seat 4.
Oblong	52" x 70" for tables that measure 28" x 46" to 40" x 58". These tables seat 4 to 6.
	60" x 84" for tables that measure 36" x 60" to 48" x 72". These tables seat 6 to 8.
	60" x 104" for a table that measures 36" x 36" to 80" x 92". These tables seat 8 to 10.
Round	60" for tables 36" diameter to 48" diameter. These tables seat 4.
	70" for tables 48" diameter to 58" diameter. These tables seat 4 to 6.
	90" for tables 66" diameter to 78" diameter. These tables will seat 4 to 6.

stocking the kitchen

The kitchen is the heart of every home—and the summer home is no exception. If you're traveling by car to a summer rental and are unsure of how well-stocked the kitchen might be, consider bringing along some basic tools of survival. Below are some things that you might forget if you're planning on cooking while away.

THE NECESSITIES

- » Coffee grinder
- » Pepper mill
- » Oyster knives/clam knives
- » Lobster crackers/nutcrackers
- » Lobster pot
- » Cheese grater
- » All-purpose chef's knife
- » Corkscrew
- » Large skillet
- » Blender
- » BBQ tools (find out first if there is a grill—if not, consider a portable hibachi)
- » Storage containers/ food storage bags / garbage bags

And don't forget for the fridge . . .

- » Bread
- » Butter
- » Eggs
- » Lemons and limes
- » Milk
- » Juice
- » Cheese

PANTRY

I like to keep the pantry filled with jarred and canned foods for when unexpected guests arrive, or when I'm simply too lazy to drive to the market to pick up groceries. A pound of cooked pasta, combined with a jar of sun-dried tomatoes, a bit of cracked pepper, and grated cheese, is a great meal that you can throw together with just a few staples. Or pulse together a can of drained chickpeas, a clove or two of garlic, and two tablespoons of olive oil in the food processor, for a simple, homemade hummus to enjoy with olives, raw veggies, and pita bread or crackers. And don't forget the Parmalat; to me, nothing is worse than waking up to find there's no milk for my morning tea!

- » Parmalat milk
- » Olive oil / flavored oils
- » Nonstick cooking spray
- » Balsamic vinegar
- » Sea salt
- » Pepper
- » Dijon mustard
- » Old Bay Seasoning
- » Bread crumbs
- » Herbes de Provence
- » Jars of roasted red peppers, olives, spreads and dips, capers, sun-dried tomatoes, marinated artichokes
- » Dried pasta, rice, cornmeal
- » Bread and assorted crackers
- » Dried fruit and nuts
- » Honey and sugar
- » Coffee and tea
- » Pancake mix and maple syrup
- » Oatmeal
- » Peanut butter
- » Jams and jellies
- » Cans of tuna, chicken stock, chickpeas, cannellini beans, anchovies, diced tomatoes, tomato paste

20 THINGS NO SUMMER HOME SHOULD BE WITHOUT

- » Sturdy canvas bag (for carrying firewood, visits to the market, trips to the beach)
- » Air mattress (for extra guests)
- » Flashlights
- » Alarm clocks
- » Extension cords (indoor and outdoor)
- » Spare batteries
- » Cooler/thermos
- » Candles
- » Sun and golf umbrella
- » Bug repellent/bug spray
- » Binoculars
- » Fly swatters
- » Ant traps
- » Disposable cameras
- » Plunger
- » Liquid clog remover (like Drano or Liquid-Plumr)
- » WD-40
- » Matches
- » Small sewing kit
- » Garbage bags

hosting weekend guests

Where I live in New York State, we tend to hibernate for a good part of the winter. In the summer months, however, everything changes, and our household springs to life with barbecues and picnics and parties. And with those festivities come house guests. For the friends who come for a day and stay for a week, I make sure the pantry is stocked with plenty of snacks and beverages, and I keep the guest room equipped with fresh, clean towels, alarm clock, water carafe or bottled water, a pen and a pad, so I don't have to scramble to get them settled in.

a few basic tips for welcoming guests

- » Spend a night in the guest room. If you're not comfortable, your guests won't be either.

- » Provide at least one empty dresser drawer and plenty of hangers in the closets.

- » Make sure there's a mirror in the room.

- » If there is room, add a comfortable chair to the guest room for lounging or reading.

- » If there is a television in the room, leave the remote and a TV listing in a visible place.

- » Give your guests a tour of the kitchen so they know where to find everything.

if you want to go all out

- » Fill a binder with sightseeing or "things to do" brochures, menus from local restaurants, movie schedules, maps.

- » Put a bouquet of wildflowers from your garden in the guest room.

- » Fill a basket with paperback novels and magazines for your guests to read.

- » Keep a supply of extra toothbrushes, sweatshirts, flip-flops, baseball caps, and warm socks for guests to use.

- » Disposable cameras are a nice way for guests to remember their stay—keep a few on hand, or leave one in their room.

what's for breakfast?

Breakfast is a meal that guests can easily make on their own, but if you want to all sit down together, here's a lovely menu to serve with coffee or tea.

challah bread vanilla french toast

Don't panic if you can't find challah bread at the market; this works just as well with raisin bread, a brioche loaf, or even a loaf of good white bread. If you want a more exotic-flavored, adult version, substitute two tablespoons of Kahlúa for the vanilla extract.

   3 large eggs

   1 cup milk

   1 tablespoon vanilla extract

   1 teaspoon sugar

   1/4 teaspoon salt

   One 1- to 1 1/2-pound challah loaf, sliced crosswise into 1/2-inch-thick slices (discard end pieces)

   2 to 4 tablespoons unsalted butter

Whisk together the eggs, milk, sugar, and salt, then pour into a large baking pan. Lay the bread slices in the egg mixture in a single layer, and soak for 2 minutes. With a spatula, carefully flip bread slices over and soak for an additional 2 minutes.

   Place 1 1/2 to 2 tablespoons of butter in a heavy skillet or griddle and melt over high heat. With your spatula, carefully transfer 2 to 3 slices of the bread to the skillet, and cook until golden brown, around 2 minutes on each side. Repeat with remaining bread, adding more butter as needed.

   Serve the French toast with warm maple syrup, fresh berry compote, or a sprinkle of granulated or confectioners' sugar. » serves 4 to 6

homemade sausage patties

Subtly flavored with maple syrup, these patties are easily thrown together in a hurry, and go wonderfully with French toast.

   1 tablespoon dried fennel seeds

   1 1/2 teaspoons salt

   1/2 teaspoon black pepper

   1 1/2 lbs. ground pork

   4 tablespoons maple syrup

   1 tablespoon olive oil or vegetable oil

In a mixing bowl, add all the ingredients except the oil and mix with your hands, a spoon, or a spatula until well combined.

   Add the oil to a skillet and place over medium-high heat.

   Divide the pork mixture into six equal portions, and with your hands, form the patties. Cook the patties for approximately 4 or 5 minutes on each side, or until browned. Drain on paper towels before serving. » serves 6

bloody mary

   2 ounces vodka

   5 ounces tomato juice

   1 dash lemon juice

   1/2 teaspoon Worcestershire sauce

   2 to 3 drops Tabasco sauce

   Ice

   Salt and pepper to taste

   1 lime wedge or celery stalk for garnish (optional)

Mix the vodka, juices, Worcestershire sauce, and Tabasco in a cocktail shaker with ice. Strain into an old-fashioned glass over ice cubes, then add salt and pepper to taste. If desired, garnish with the lime wedge or celery stalk. » serves 1

HOW TO be the perfect house guest

It goes both ways. If you're fortunate enough to have friends who welcome you into their home, there are rules you should follow if you want to be invited back! While it goes without saying that you shouldn't bring your drum set or your six cats along, there are a few things you might not have considered:

» Rule number one: Don't show up unexpectedly. And never show up with an uninvited friend or date.

» Let your hosts know when you'll be arriving and departing, and let them in on any specific plans you have, or dietary needs.

» Don't expect your hosts to supply your health and beauty aids. Pack everything you'll need, from sunscreen to shampoo, to survive your stay.

» You're not staying at a hotel, and your host isn't your maid. Make your bed, keep your living space neat and tidy, and clean up any messes you make.

» Chip in for groceries, movie rentals, and gas. Help around the house by offering to cook. If your host and hostess are gracious enough to make your meals, offer to set the table, help with food preparations, or clean up.

» Don't expect your host to be your personal chauffeur, and don't assume that his car is your car. You can always rent a car, moped, or bike; hop on a bus; or call a taxi.

» When your stay is over, offer to wash the linens and towels you've used. Give your room and the bathroom you've used a once-over to make sure everything is the way it was when you arrived.

» Leave a thank-you note in an unexpected place for your host to discover after you're gone. I've left notes in refrigerators, the newspaper, and even slippers! If you forget, you can always show your appreciation by sending a note or calling within three or four days.

» Bring more than just your luggage: good house guests come with stories to tell, ideas for what they'd like to do, and enthusiasm. Be adventurous and go with the flow.

» Give your hosts the space they need. Take a walk or a drive, offer to go food shopping, or keep yourself amused.

HOUSE GUESTS BEARING GIFTS

While bringing a gift is certainly not a necessity, it is a nice gesture that shows your host you appreciate his or her generosity. If you planned on getting one but simply didn't have the time, send a gift no more than three days after your departure. Here are some ideas you might not have thought of:

» A lawn game such as croquet, badminton, or bocce, a collection of rainy-day DVDs, or a new board game.

» A colorful raft or float makes a great gift if they have a pool or live by a lake.

» For bird lovers, an Audubon book, an interesting birdfeeder or birdhouse, or a pair of binoculars.

» Hand-blown margarita glasses and matching pitcher, or a hand-painted serving tray.

» An addition to the yard or garden, such as a plant, wind chimes, a garden sculpture, a gazing ball, or a hammock (with an offer to help hang it).

» Flavored oils and vinegars, a homemade jam or pesto.

» This book!

the fourth of july

Smack dab between Memorial Day and Labor Day lies *the* American holiday, the Fourth of July. In small towns and big cities alike, flags are hoisted, parades march down Main Street, sparklers are lit, and fireworks paint the night sky bright.

The most spectacular of these celebrations is the famous Macy's fireworks display in New York City. For more than a quarter of a century this spectacle, by even the lofty standards of jaded New Yorkers, deploys fifty times the firepower of most civic fireworks displays. Launched from barges in the East River, more than 30,000 pyrotechnic shells dazzle millions of city dwellers and countless others tuning in around the world.

A less famous New York tradition is the Nathan's Famous Fourth of July International Hot Dog Eating Contest. Each summer since 1916, iron-stomached contestants have lined up at Nathan's in Coney Island for a shot at the title. As of July 4, 2006, 131-pound Takeru "the Tsunami" Kobayashi of Japan holds the record, having consumed $53\frac{3}{4}$ hot dogs in only 12 minutes. We Americans have set our own hot dog eating records on that day as well: we devour 16 billion franks on average each year, and more than 150 million on the Fourth of July alone!

our national anthem

A recent poll found that two out of three Americans didn't know the words to "The Star-Spangled Banner." For those who want to practice for the next Fourth or ball game, I present the words to the first stanza.

O say, can you see, by the dawn's early light,
What so proudly we hailed at the twilight's last gleaming?
Whose broad stripes and bright stars, through the perilous fight;
O'er the ramparts we watched, were so gallantly streaming!
And the rockets' red glare, the bombs bursting in air,
Gave proof through the night that our flag was still there.
O say, does that Star-Spangled Banner yet wave
O'er the land of the free, and the home of the brave?

FLAG ETIQUETTE

» The stars should be located on the upper left-hand side. Fly the flag upside down only as a distress signal.

» Raise the flag briskly and lower it ceremoniously.

» On Memorial Day, the flag should be hung at half-staff until noon, when it should be raised to the top of the staff.

» Never allow the flag to touch the ground.

» Fly the flag after dark only if properly illuminated.

» Don't display the flag in inclement weather unless it is an all-weather flag.

» When not on display, the flag should be folded neatly.

» A damaged flag should be destroyed by burning.

20 easy appetizers

The key to being able to invite guests over on the spur of the moment—and feed them—is to have a couple of tried-and-true recipes that you're confident will work perfectly. Here are twenty of mine.

1 Serve slices of **smoked duck breast** or smoked breast of chicken with hot pepper jelly and assorted crackers.

2 Make **quesadillas** by placing four 6-inch flour tortillas on a medium-heat grill. Sprinkle half the tortilla with some diced Brie (omit rind), chopped mango, and diced red onion. Fold in half over the filling, press down lightly, and grill for 1 to 2 minutes on each side, or until they're golden brown and the cheese has melted. Cut into wedges and serve with sour cream and fruit salsa. (For traditional quesadillas, fill with Cheddar cheese, chopped cilantro, chopped scallions, and diced chicken or chorizo. Top with salsa and sour cream.)

3 Grab a few bags of edamame (young soybeans) from the frozen food section of your market, then boil them in salted water. When they're done, sprinkle with coarse salt and serve with cold sake or saketinis.

4 Wrap pitted dates or shrimp or whole water chestnuts in half a slice of bacon, secure with a toothpick, and bake until golden.

5 Serve smoked salmon and/or smoked trout with horseradish cream (mix sour cream and horseradish together to taste), capers, and diced onion. Serve on water crackers.

6 Skewer some peeled shrimp, rub them with olive oil and crushed garlic, and grill for 2 to 3 minutes on each side. Serve the **kabobs** with lemon wedges.

7 For a yummy, summery spread, drain a small jar of oil-packed sun-dried tomatoes and process in a food processor until fine. Add goat cheese and blend until smooth. Serve with assorted crackers.

8 To make a **garlicky escargot** appetizer, blend together 1 tablespoon of minced garlic, 1 tablespoon of chopped parsley, 1 tablespoon of white wine, and 1 stick ($\frac{1}{2}$ cup) of butter. Spread 12 to 24 canned snails in a baking dish, top them with the garlic paste, then bake for 4 to 6 minutes. Serve with slices of crusty bread for dipping.

9 Hollow out cherry tomatoes and stuff with Boursin cheese, or fresh crab salad.

10 Top balls of **fresh mozzarella** with a splash of good olive oil and some shredded fresh basil leaves. Serve them over roasted red peppers with garlicky toasts on the side.

11 Make Parmesan pita crisps by splitting six pitas in half horizontally, then brush the insides with $\frac{1}{4}$ cup of olive oil. Cut each round into eight slices, sprinkle with $1\frac{1}{2}$ cups of Parmesan cheese, and top with a twist or two of freshly ground pepper. Bake at 375°F. for 12 to 15 minutes, or until golden.

12 Everyone loves **vegetable crudités**. Purchase precleaned vegetables from the market, or pick fresh veggies from your garden, and serve with a creamy dip. To make a simple dip, combine $\frac{3}{4}$ cup of sour cream, $\frac{1}{2}$ cup of mayonnaise, $\frac{1}{3}$ cup each of chopped parsley and chopped fresh chives, $\frac{1}{4}$ teaspoon minced garlic, salt, and pepper.

13 For cheesy bread sticks, dip thin strips of refrigerated bread stick dough into a mixture of $\frac{1}{4}$ cup grated Parmesan cheese, $\frac{1}{3}$ cup grated Gruyère cheese, and 1 teaspoon chopped fresh rosemary. Twist the sticks, then place on a parchment-lined baking sheet, and bake in a preheated 350°F. oven until golden brown (approximately 10 to 15 minutes).

14 Pick up some pâtés and terrines at the market. Serve with cornichons, capers, a selection of mustards, and assorted crackers and toasts.

15 To make sausage balls, mix together 1 cup grated sharp Cheddar cheese, 1 pound bulk sausage, and 2 cups Bisquick. Roll into small balls, place on a cookie sheet, and bake in a preheated 400°F. oven for 10 minutes. Serve warm.

16 Make goat cheese toasts by slicing a loaf of French bread into ⅓-inch-thick rounds, then broil for 1 to 2 minutes on each side, or until they're golden. Remove from the broiler, brush with olive oil, sprinkle with crumbled goat cheese, and top with a twist or two of cracked pepper. Broil until the cheese melts (approximately 1 minute), then serve.

17 Drizzle 1 cup of honey over 4 ounces of feta cheese. Sprinkle with cracked pepper and serve with assorted crackers.

18 Sauté whole button mushrooms in olive oil and lots of minced garlic. Add a squirt of lemon, some chopped parsley, and a twist of black pepper before serving with toasts.

19 Create a delicious tapenade by combining 1 cup pitted Kalamata olives, 2 anchovies (rinsed and patted dry), 1 clove garlic, 1 tablespoon capers, and the zest and juice of 1 lemon in a food processor. Pulse until the mixture becomes a paste. Gradually add ¼ cup of olive oil until blended. Season with salt and pepper. Serve with vegetable crudités and crackers.

20 When you need to impress a special guest but are short on time, head to the market and pick up some American caviar (from paddlefish or Atlantic sturgeon); it's not only considerably more affordable than Russian or Iranian caviar, but it can hold its own on taste and texture. Serve it with toast points or blini, a bit of chopped egg, and some crème fraîche. Add some oysters and champagne, and the evening will be a 10 out of 10.

summer pesto

This fresh basil sauce is perfect for spreading on grilled toasts, mixing into warm pasta, as a pizza topping, or to add flavor to Italian soups.

- **4 cups fresh basil leaves, well packed**
- **4 cloves garlic, lightly crushed and peeled**
- **1 cup pine nuts or walnuts (or a combination of the two), lightly toasted if you prefer**
- **1½ cups freshly grated Parmigiano-Reggiano or Pecorino cheese (or a combination of the two)**
- **1 to 1½ cups olive oil**
- **Salt and pepper to taste**

Place the basil leaves, garlic, and nuts in a food processor and pulse until finely chopped. Add the cheese and process until combined.

While the machine is still running, slowly add the olive oil and salt and pepper.

Store the pesto in an airtight container with a thin coating of olive oil on top to keep the sauce from turning brown. The pesto will keep well in the refrigerator for about a week. If you want to freeze batches of the pesto, omit the cheese; you can add it once it's thawed. **» makes about 3 cups**

There's a well-worn path that leads from the front door of my home to an old magnolia tree in the yard. Tucked beneath its canopy of leaves are two roomy Adirondack chairs, painted white but weathered by time and use. Every summer morning that I'm home, I head to this peaceful spot and sit quietly with a cup of tea, listening as the chickadees, woodpeckers, and mourning doves welcome a fresh new day. Occasionally, one of the many deer that roam the surrounding woods passes by, too sleepy to notice me, or a bunny will pop out of its burrow, looking nervously at the harrier circling above. It's in these chairs that we have sat, bundled up at ungodly hours, watching the miracle of the Perseid meteor showers light the sky above, and more golden sunsets than I can even begin to count.

The classic chair of summer, named for the Adirondack mountains of upstate New York where it originated, has been around since the early 1900s. As legend has it, a Mr. Thomas Lee, unhappy with the uninspired outdoor seating at his summer home in Westport, set to work on creating a comfortable and stylish lawn chair of his own. He handcrafted his "Westport plank chair," with its trademark wide armrests, from eleven pieces of wood, all cut from a single board. Good-hearted soul that Lee was, he then offered the design to Harry Bunnell, a carpenter friend in need of winter income. The proverbial lightbulb went off in Bunnell's head as he realized the chair was the perfect item to market to summer residents, so—clearly less interested in an enduring friendship than in a substantial livelihood—the carpenter filed for and received a patent for the chair in 1904. While the length of their friendship remains a mystery, the longevity of their chair does not; today's version has been modified slightly for ergonomics and aesthetics (it is now offered in a rainbow of colors) but it is otherwise unchanged since its introduction more than a century ago.

HOW TO line-dry summer linens

At night, slip between crisp sheets and pillowcases that smell of mowed grass and lilies of the valley and pine—the smell of nature itself. Here are some tips for line-drying clothes.

scented linen water

If you can't hang your linens out to dry, infuse them with the sweet summery scent of flowers or herbs. Spray this lightly scented water on your sheets and pillowcases before ironing; spray on sheets to freshen up the bed between washings, or use as a room spray.

10 to 20 drops (or more, depending on your preference) of lavender, peppermint, rosemary, spearmint, rose, jasmine, or any other essential oil with a summery scent

3 ounces nonflavored high proof (80+) vodka

Spray bottle (sterilize with boiling water before using)

25 ounces distilled water

Pour the essential oil and vodka into a spray bottle and shake well until they are thoroughly mixed, then add the distilled water. Shake well before each use.

» Use a good-quality clothesline so it won't sag.

» Birds like to perch on clotheslines, so every few weeks, dip a clean rag in a mixture of Pine-Sol (or another pine-oil-based cleanser) and warm water and wipe off any droppings that can stain clothes.

» Make sure your clothespins are clean and snag-free. To clean them, place them in a mesh bag and let soak in warm sudsy water for 5 minutes, then rinse and hang on the line to dry.

» Fold the sheets in half, hem to hem, then turn about three or four inches over the line and pin.

» Don't hang towels by the corners or they'll develop permanent indentations. Simply fold them over the line; once they're dry, shake them out to fluff them up.

» Fold men's shirts in half by bringing the two shirtfronts together. Hang by the tail, folding three or four inches over the line and pinning at the ends.

» Hang dresses and pants or any items you want to hold in their original shape on hangers, then secure the hanger to the line.

THE OUTDOOR SHOWER

Every sunny day from June to September, I head to a private spot in our garden where we've set up a simple outdoor shower. It's nothing more than a slotted cedar plank platform, a squeaky hinged door for privacy, a few hooks for hanging towels, and an oversized showerhead that pours a warm rain shower down upon me, but it's one of my favorite places. All winter I look forward to the feeling of warm, fresh air on my skin and the sound of bees buzzing in the sweet honeysuckle nearby.

In Botswana a few years back, I took advantage of the outdoor showers at our camps; it was over 100 degrees on most days, so a cool shower at the end of the day was a welcome treat. More times than not, a mischievous baboon would be eyeing me from a nearby branch, waiting for me to turn my back so he could steal my soap. In fact, those baboons have gotten so clever that they've learned to turn the showers on themselves. It seems that even primates love washing in the great outdoors.

RESOURCES

If you're interested in setting up a backyard shower, consult:

Calazzo
Tel.: 1-480-993-2228;
www.calazzo.com

Rittenhouse
Tel.: 1-877-488-1914;
www.rittenhouse.ca

Specialty Pool Products
Tel.: 1-800-983-7665;
www.poolproducts.com

summer salt glow scrub

After a long day at the beach or in the woods, exfoliate your dry, tired summer skin with this rejuvenating salt scrub. Make an extra batch to give as a lovely hostess gift.

Large, wide-mouthed glass jar with lid (sterilize with boiling water before using)

2 cups sea salt

2 cups apricot, almond, or grapeseed oil

15 (more or less) drops of an essential oil (Try coconut- or ocean-scented oils if you're near the beach; rainwater-, pine-, or wildflower-scented oils for the woods or lake.)

Place the salt in the jar and cover with the oil. Add the desired amount of essential oil and mix well.

Stir to combine the ingredients, then dampen your entire body and massage into the skin using circular motions. Do not use the scrub on your face or on scratched or cut areas.

Rinse off with warm water. Your skin will be smooth and soft and gently scented.

GROWING A kitchen herb garden

A kitchen garden created exclusively for herbs is simple to build and will reward you with wonderful aromas and delicious flavors all summer long. Herbs are a valuable addition to so many dishes. Below are a few of the favorites that are easy to grow.

basil To harvest, pinch or cut the leaves off from the top; if you need whole stems, cut just above a pair of leaves. When your plant begins to produce flowers, pinch them off to encourage leafy growth. Dry your basil for winter cooking by hanging small bunches upside down in a dry, well-ventilated room for about a week. You can also freeze the leaves by placing small batches in airtight bags and storing in the freezer.

I add basil to practically everything, from Italian classics like pesto and pizza, to Asian dishes like pad thai and basil beef. I especially love it on fresh mozzarella and tomato sandwiches.

chives One of the easiest herbs to grow, these perennials prefer a partially sunny spot that has good drainage. Harvest chives by giving them a "haircut"; if you don't cut your plant back on a regular basis, it will eventually produce purple flowers (which isn't a catastrophe because the flowers are edible and can be added to salads for both color and flavor). Chives are one of those herbs that simply don't dry well, so to preserve for the off-season, just chop them, place them in ice-cube trays with a bit of water, and freeze. When you're ready to use, just defrost.

cilantro Also called Chinese parsley, the annual cilantro looks like parsley and is used in Mexican, Caribbean, and Asian cooking, although its claim to fame is as a key ingredient in salsa. Cilantro is a fussy herb that doesn't last very long in the garden, so plan to reseed every 3 to 4 weeks in order to have a patch growing all summer long. To harvest, pinch the fresh leaves regularly.

Unfortunately, it doesn't dry well, so try to use what you harvest—throw some leaves into your Brie and mango quesadillas, mix them into a watermelon salsa, shred them into Asian coleslaw—or freeze them in airtight containers for 2 to 6 months.

dill One of the easiest herbs to raise, dill can grow up to 3 feet tall, so take that into consideration when choosing a container or a space in your garden (you might want to plant it toward the back). Harvest it regularly to prevent the plant from going to seed; if you cut more than you can use, simply dry it to use later on: spread it in a single layer on a paper towel and microwave on high for 3 minutes, then discard the stems, crumble the leaves, and store in an airtight container at room temperature.

HERB GARDEN TIPS

» There are two types of herbs—perennials and annuals. Perennial herbs grow for more than one season. Annual herbs complete their life cycle in one year. Decide what herbs you would like to grow, then separate the annuals from the perennials to facilitate harvesting and replanting.

» Most herbs that get six to eight hours of sun a day are more robust, so pick a sunny spot near the kitchen, or use containers that can be readily repositioned to follow the sun.

» Make sure your planting area has good drainage. Add a bit of compost or fertilizer to the soil before planting. Plant herbs approximately 18 inches apart.

» Once the herbs begin to grow, harvest the leaves and shoots regularly to encourage new growth.

» Herbs harvested in the morning have the most flavor.

mint This herb requires no work at all—chances are it will take over your entire garden by summer's end. Grow it in pots to contain it, then place in a partially shaded spot and water regularly. The smell reminds me of my childhood home, where it grew wild just about everywhere (despite admirable, but futile attempts by my mother to weed it out).

There are more than thirty species of mint, although most gardeners grow the basics like spearmint or peppermint. I like to add some more exotic varieties to my garden such as bergamot mint or chocolate peppermint for desserts. Add mint to flavor both hot and cold teas, muddle it into mojitos, sprinkle over fresh peas, or simply chew on a leaf or two to help ease indigestion or freshen your breath.

oregano Oregano is an important ingredient in Italian cooking, but it plays a key role in the foods of Greece as well. Often confused with marjoram (it's in the same family), oregano is a strong-flavored herb that is best used in moderation and added during the final stages of cooking. Make sure it receives at least 5 hours of sunlight each day, and allow the soil to dry between waterings. Harvest the leaves when the plant has reached 4 to 5 inches, keeping in mind that once the plant blooms, the levels of essential oils diminish. To dry, tie cuttings in small bunches, then hang upside down in a well-ventilated room for a week or so.

rosemary This evergreen shrub, a member of the mint family, adds a wonderful pinelike fragrance to your garden and a lovely flavor to foods. This perennial can grow up to 6 feet tall, so make sure there's plenty of room for it to flourish, then offer it lots of full sunlight.

We eat rosemary potatoes until the cows come home and I love rubbing it on lamb or pork with a little olive oil, salt, and pepper before grilling the meat. Try adding it to homemade breads, or mix it with some good olive oil for a delicious dipping sauce.

sage Sage has a strong flavor, which often overpowers foods. But just a small bit goes a long way in vinaigrettes, marinades, and sauces. I use it on my famous (at least in my house they are) grilled pizzas and to add flavor to my homemade sausage. Once I even spent the better part of an afternoon making sage jelly to accompany a delicious grilled leg of lamb. Fairly hardy, sage is tolerant of almost all conditions as long as it gets plenty of sunlight; don't overwater, it actually prefers its soil on the dry side. To harvest this perennial, simply pinch off a few leaves when needed. You can also freeze sage in resealable plastic bags, or dry it (see Dill opposite) and store in airtight containers.

tarragon I haven't met a vinegar yet that isn't radically improved by the addition of tarragon, and its mild anise flavor goes well with vinaigrettes, flavorful béarnaise sauces, and Dijon mustards. It's a headachy little perennial that can be difficult to grow, but it's worth the effort. Give it plenty of sunshine, but don't overwater since it's susceptible to root rot. To harvest, pinch off a few leaves before using, or dry or freeze for use down the road. Add it to your Sunday morning omelets, sprinkle over salads, or make tarragon mayonnaise (mix ¾ cup mayo, ¼ cup minced tarragon, and 4 teaspoons of tarragon vinegar) to spread on grilled chicken sandwiches to add a lovely flavor.

thyme Thyme is another one of those strong, pungent herbs that should be used with restraint. But don't let that scare you away from growing it in your garden and cooking with it in your kitchen. A member of the mint family, this perennial does best in hot, dry climates, so give it plenty of sun and water it once or twice per week. To harvest, just pinch or cut the leaves as needed; remove and discard any flower clusters that may bloom.

I like to add some thyme to my homemade breads, especially focaccia, as well as to sweet lemon cookies and roasted chicken. And I make a celery root bisque that goes from good to great with the addition of a few crunchy thyme croutons. Don't be afraid to experiment with it in your summer-house kitchen.

FLIP-FLOPS

As close as you can get to bare feet, flip-flops are an essential part of the relaxed summer lifestyle. I wear my Reefs—the Rolls-Royce of flip-flops—from when the first crocuses pop up in early spring until the chilly days of late autumn, when practicality wins out.

Sandals were the very first shoes known to man. Our Stone Age ancestors fashioned them from animal skins to protect their feet from sharp rocks and thorns. The Ancient Egyptians made them from papyrus, palm leaves, and even rawhide and wood. Wooden sandals were popular in India, rice straw sandals were the fashion in China and Japan, and sisal plant sandals caught on in South America.

The Japanese call sandals zori; in New Zealand they're called jandals (from "Japanese sandals"). We call them "flip-flops," a name derived from the rhythmic slapping sound that the sandals make while walking.

flowery flip-flops

Brightly colored silk flowers add color and whimsy to everyday flip-flops.

Wire cutters
Silk flowers
Strong adhesive glue
Flip-flops

1. With wire cutters, clip a flower from its stem (some silk flowers simply pop off). If some of the petals loosen, simply glue them back together.

2. Squeeze a bit of glue onto the back of your flower, press it firmly onto the top of your flip-flop, and hold it in place until the glue has hardened.

3. Repeat this process for the other flip-flop.

the perfect pedicure

When wearing flip-flops or any other kind of sandals, it's important that your feet look good! Here's how to put your best foot forward.

1. Remove any old nail polish with cotton balls dipped in nail polish remover.

2. Soak your feet in warm, soapy water for 10 to 15 minutes. For an extra treat, add ½ cup of Epsom salts to help absorb foot odors and soften rough skin. Use a loofah or pumice stone to smooth roughened or callused areas.

3. Dry your feet with a clean towel.

4. With a nail clipper, clip your toenails straight across (which helps prevent ingrown nails), and file your toenails to smooth any sharp or rough edges.

5. Using a wooden cuticle stick, gently push back your cuticles from the nail. If you have dry, stubborn cuticles, a cuticle cream (such as Burt's Bees Lemon Butter Cuticle Cream) will help soften them up.

6. Massage your feet with a rich moisturizing lotion.

7. If you are going to paint your toenails, separate your toes by placing pieces of cotton between them, or purchase one of those handy foam separators from the drugstore. Clean nails again with polish remover, to remove any residual moisturizer, then apply a clear base coat. Allow to dry. Carefully apply nail polish to toenails in even strokes. If some color gets onto your skin, simply remove it with a cotton swab dipped in polish remover. Allow polish to dry, then add a second coat for deeper color.

8. To add extra strength and resilience, finish your pedicure with a top coat of clear polish.

HOW TO arrange flowers

For those of us happiest out in the garden with our hands in the soil, arranging our own flowers is a joy. For those new to flower arranging, here are a few simple tips:

» Fill a vase with cool water and a few drops of bleach (or floral food) to extend the life of your flowers. Pick the right size vase for the quantity of flowers you're using, so the arrangement doesn't look overcrowded or sparse.

» Remove all leaves that will be underwater (they will rot and shorten the life of your flowers).

» With a sharp knife, cut the flower stems at a deep angle so that the flower is able to take in more water.

» Crisscross the stems of taller flowers to help anchor the arrangement in place. When adding flowers, place taller ones in the center and shorter ones closer to the rim. Mix flowers with different shapes, colors, and textures.

» Combine flowers at various stages of opening—tight buds, half-open, and fully open flowers—this really looks dramatic!

» Keep cut flowers in a cool room if possible, and far away from direct sun.

» Changing the water every day and rinsing the stems under water will ensure your flowers live as long as possible.

GET CREATIVE

Here are some summer-inspired containers to show off your favorite flowers. You can use objects that can't hold water by placing a jar or plastic tub inside.

» Colorful pitchers

» Old bottles (if you need to, remove the top with a glass cutter)

» Rustic baskets

» Mason jars

» Tin cans

» Champagne flutes

» Cocktail shakers

» Watering cans

» Rubber rain boots

» Plastic buckets

The sunflower isn't a single flower, but a cluster of more than two thousand tiny ones.

HOW TO grow sunflowers

Perhaps it's their bright, shining faces, or the ridiculous heights they reach, but sunflowers have a way of making us feel happier.

» After all danger of frost has passed, find a sunny patch in your yard.

» Plant the seeds 1 inch deep and 1 to 2 feet apart and water just enough to keep the soil moist.

» Trim the spent blooms to encourage more flowers.

roasted sunflower seeds

1 cup sunflower seeds
2 quarts water
½ cup salt

Rinse the sunflower seeds and remove any plant and flower matter.

Put the seeds, water, and salt in a saucepan and bring to a boil, then lower the heat and simmer for 1 to 1½ hours. When done, drain the seeds on paper towels until dry. Do not rinse.

Preheat the oven to 325°F. Spread the seeds on a cookie sheet and bake for 25 to 30 minutes, mixing frequently. Remove from the oven when they turn slightly brown. Allow your seeds to cool before eating. » serves 2 to 3

Note » For added zip, try sprinkling a bit of onion, garlic, or chili powder on the seeds before roasting.

Once seen on nearly every porch in small-town U.S.A., porch swings evoke longings for a slower-paced past—a place where families and friends chatted away in the evening, a place where young couples held hands, a place where skinned knees were kissed away, where memories were made. Porch swings have been immortalized in movies, music, poems, and art. Who can forget Atticus Finch in *To Kill a Mockingbird,* sitting on his porch swing, listening to Scout and Jem talk about their late mother as they fall asleep? Elton John sang about a "Porch Swing in Tupelo," while Dolly Parton serenaded us with "Sittin' on the Front Porch Swing." There's also a little rhyme that seems to capture the Norman Rockwell spirit of the porch swing perfectly:

Sitting on the porch swing,
Going to and fro,
Watching all the people,
Feeling breezes blow.

bird-watching FOR BEGINNERS

We're lucky enough to live on a large country property, so wildlife is in great abundance here, and our bird population grows larger with each passing year. In addition to the "regulars," this year we spotted several red-tailed hawks flying over the yard, as well as a family of turkeys making their way single file across the lawn. If you're feeling adventurous this summer, bird-watching is an easy, inexpensive, and relaxing way to enjoy nature.

With over 926 species of birds in North America, a good guidebook is essential. I like the National Audubon Society's field guide (choose the correct one for your region), or *The Sibley Guide to Birds.*

You'll need a decent pair of binoculars to view birds from a distance, but always locate a bird first with your naked eye because binoculars have a narrower field of vision.

Find a place where you can observe birds in their natural environment, such as a park, forest, nature preserve, or your own backyard.

To identify a bird, there are a few things to take into consideration:

» Note the basic shape and size of the bird (use a reference object like a tree, shrub, fence post to help determine size).

» See if there is anything unique about the shape of the birds wings, beak, or feet.

» Can you spot any special colors and markings on the bird?

» What is the habitat of the bird? Is it near the water, or in the trees?

» Can you hear its call or song? (Refer to your field guide as they usually have bird calls phonetically spelled out.)

» How does the bird feed/eat?

» Always keep a journal where you can record details. Make a sketch or two if it will help you identify the bird later on, or if you have a camera with a zoom lens, try snapping a few shots.

what not to do

» Don't disturb birds that are nesting or eggs in nests.

» Don't take pets with you as they can scare birds away.

» Don't disturb a bird's natural ecosystem.

CREATING A bird-friendly backyard

I always know we've turned the corner on winter when—just around daybreak—I hear the familiar tune of songbirds outside our bedroom window. Offer them food, water, and shelter, and you'll be rewarded with their sweet song all summer long.

feeding

» Different types of birds like different types of foods. Finches, cardinals, nuthatches, chickadees, and grosbeaks like black oil sunflower seeds; indigo buntings go for millet; goldfinches love thistle seed; and woodpeckers pine for suet. For this reason—and because aggressive birds like blue jays often scare away smaller birds—you may want to set up several feeders around your yard: larger ones for bigger birds and smaller ones with small perches for the little guys.

» Hang your feeder away from fences, trees, bushes, tall grasses, and patio furniture; this will give birds a better view of predators. Some birds, such as juncos, doves, towhees, and cardinals, prefer to feed on or near the ground, so you could spread some seed there as well. Store your birdseed in a cool, dry place; mold can be harmful to birds.

gimme shelter

» Birds frequent areas with lots of trees where they can rest safely. By planting flowers or fruit bushes beneath the trees, you can supplement their food supply. Evergreen trees provide shelter to many types of birds in the winter months.

» Birdhouses are fairly inexpensive to purchase (and easy to make if you're so inclined) and offer a safe spot for birds to roost. Not all backyard birds use houses—cardinals, orioles, and goldfinches don't, for example—but enough do nest in them to make it worthwhile to set up a few. We have several, including one made from a coconut shell on the front porch, where I often hear the insistent sound of hungry, chirping chicks.

» You can also provide nesting material for your birds to make it easier for them to build their own homes. Short pieces of thread or string, wood chips, dryer lint, and pretty much anything else that is stringy or soft is perfect. Clip the pieces to about 2 inches in length, so they're easy for the birds to handle.

the 2-minute birdbath

Birds need to bathe and drink, so a birdbath is a big added enticement for birds to stop by.

To make this simple one, overturn two terra-cotta pots of slightly different sizes (for example, a 12-inch pot and a 16-inch pot), stack them in a special spot in your yard or garden (where predators can't hide), then top with a large terra-cotta saucer. Fill with cool fresh water.

Nobody likes swimming in dirty water, birds included. Stagnant water is not only unhealthy, but it's also a breeding ground for mosquitoes. The best way to clean a birdbath is the old-fashioned way—by hand. Remove the existing water and clean the bowl with a small scrub brush. Avoid harsh detergents and chemicals, but if it's heavily soiled, try using a mild detergent; just make sure you hose it out well afterward. Since birds drink and bathe in the same place, make sure to change the water on a daily basis so they keep visiting.

attracting hummingbirds

These tiny creatures can flap their wings at a rate of more than fifty-five times per second and can fly at speeds of 25 miles per hour. They're fascinating to watch—they have the ability to hover in place, fly straight up and down, move backward in the air, and even fly upside down.

If you're interested in creating an attractive environment for hummingbirds, the easiest way is to offer them their favorite food—nectar. Most hummingbirds are migratory, stopping to visit North America once the weather warms up, so do some research to find out when they arrive in your state (see Resources, at right). Once you know the approximate time of year, you can entice them with flowers and shrubs or set up a hummingbird feeder:

» To make your own nectar for a feeder, combine 1 part sugar and 4 parts water, and boil for 1 to 2 minutes. Cool, then store in the refrigerator until ready to use. (Never use honey, artificial sweeteners, or red dye as they can harm the birds.)

» Set up the feeder about 5 to 10 days in advance of the birds' estimated arrival date, so you won't miss them. Fill it just halfway; the birds won't be able to drink it all before the feeder needs to be cleaned (see below) and the nectar changed.

» To make the feeder more inviting, hang it among their favorite flowers and shrubs, or near a hanging flower basket. Since hummingbirds are attracted to the color red, try tying a red ribbon to the feeder as well. If you live in the eastern part of the country, chances are that only the ruby-throated hummingbird will visit your feeder. These birds are very territorial and defend both their flowers and feeder, so if you want to attract more than one kind of hummingbird, place additional feeders out of sight from one another.

» Clean the feeder with hot water; avoid harsh detergents. Black spots indicate mold; scrub them out with a bottle brush. Change the nectar every 3 to 4 days, more often if it's very hot outside.

» Ants love the sugary nectar as much as hummingbirds do. If they're invading your feeder, purchase an ant guard from your local Audubon store or garden center. This device attaches to the top of the feeder and really deters ants.

FLOWERS THAT ATTRACT HUMMINGBIRDS

» Begonia	» Hollyhock
» Cardinal flower	» Impatiens
» Coralbell	» Lantana
» Fuchsia	» Petunia
» Geranium	

SHRUBS AND TREES THAT ATTRACT HUMMINGBIRDS

» Azalea	» Honeysuckle
» Butterfly bush	» Morning glory
» Flowering quince	

RESOURCES

For more information on these amazing creatures, try:

The Hummingbird Society
249 East Main Street
Suite 9
P.O. Box 394
Newark, DE 19715
Tel. 1-800-529-3699
www.hummingbirdsociety.org

Hummingbirds.net
www.hummingbirds.net

Hummingbirdworld
www.hummingbirdworld.com

make a pinecone bird feeder

Strong twine

A large, open pinecone, dried (see below)

Vegetable shortening or peanut butter

Birdseed (or oats, sunflower seeds, or millet)

1. Tie a length of twine to one end of your pinecone for hanging.

2. Coat the pinecone and fill the petal openings with the shortening or peanut butter. Cover with birdseed, oats, sunflower seeds, or millet—or a combination of each.

3. Suspend from tree branches around the yard.

DRYING PINECONES

Pinecones

Aluminum foil

Cookie sheet

1. Preheat the oven to 175° to 200°F. (the lower the temperature setting at which the pinecones dry, the less brittle they will be).

2. Spread the pinecones on a foil-lined cookie sheet and place in the oven. After approximately 1 to 2 hours, the pinecones will have opened and will be dried. Allow to cool before handling.

HOW TO lure butterflies to your garden

To attract fluttering friends to your yard, you'll need to create a "butterfly friendly" environment.

» Make sure your garden gets plenty of sunshine from mid-morning to mid-afternoon, since butterflies prefer to feed in sunny spots. And provide them with nectar, either through plants or a butterfly feeder.

» Butterflies drink, so provide a source of water—a shallow saucer or a birdbath. They also need to raise their body temperature in the morning before they're capable of flying; the addition of several flat rocks in a sunny garden location makes a nice basking spot for them to warm up. Also, keep in mind that insecticides kill insects, butterflies included—don't use them near your butterfly garden.

BUTTERFLIES' FLOWERS

» Aster	» Coreopsis
» Bergamot and horsemint	» Daisy
	» Lilac
» Black-eyed Susan	» Marigold
» Blazing star	» Milkweed
» Blueberry, huckleberry	» Phlox
» Butterfly bush	» Rose verbena
» Coneflower	» Spearmint
	» Zinnia

make a simple butterfly feeder

This delicious nectar will draw butterflies into your garden, while the easy-to-make butterfly feeder keeps freeloading bugs out.

Sugar

Water

Silk flowers

Small glass jar with lid (a jelly jar or baby-food jar work well)

Strong adhesive glue or glue gun

Awl and hammer

Cotton

Tape

Length of string or twine

1. Make the butterfly nectar by combining 1 part sugar and 9 parts water.

2. Glue silk flowers onto the outside of the jar and to the lid to attract butterflies.

3. Poke a small hole in the lid of the jar with an awl and hammer. Fill the jar with butterfly nectar, then screw the lid tightly onto the jar and poke a small piece of cotton into the hole.

4. Invert the jar, tape the length of string to the bottom, and hang it in a sunny corner of your garden.

The original name for the butterfly was "flutterby."

In our backyard, strung between two tall elms, is a rope hammock that we lugged back from South Carolina a few years ago. Hand-woven and surprisingly sturdy, it holds two people. We sometimes climb in for a nap in the afternoon or use it for star gazing at night. We have had the occasional guest who's had a drink too many at our yearly summer barbecue attempt to climb in, with comedic results. And once I looked out the window and my neighbor's dog was peacefully snoring away in it, leading me to believe that neither man nor beast can resist its allure.

The hammock has come a long way through the centuries. The earliest ones were crafted from tree bark by the people of South and Central America. It didn't take long before the sisal plant became the fiber of choice; it was more abundant, and its fibers could be softened to make it easier on the skin. Eventually, someone thought of using fabric, which worked fine (and still does). In 1889, a Captain Joshua John Ward, in charge of a riverboat off Pawleys Island, South Carolina, came up with the idea of substituting rope. He was unhappy with his grass-filled mattress, so he created a comfortable hammock consisting of a web of knotted ropes separated by wooden spacers. His design caught on, and is in use today worldwide.

HOW TO hang a hammock

Hammock

Nylon rope

Heavy-duty "S" hooks (optional)

Additional chain links as necessary

Pillow (optional)

1. To hang a hammock between two trees, make sure the trunks are at least 6 inches in diameter; if you plan to hang your hammock between wooden posts, they should be at least 4 inches in diameter.

2. Plan to hang your hammock in a space between trees or poles that is about 1 foot wider than the length of the hammock itself, and to attach the hammock about 6 feet or so above the ground.

3. Use nylon rope to hang the hammock. Nylon may not have the classic look of heavy jute, but it's much easier to work with and won't stretch or mildew as easily.

4. Loop a nylon rope around the tree trunk, preferably above a crotch to hold it in place. Secure the rope with a half hitch knot (see How to Tie a Sturdy Knot, page 80) and then attach the hammock to the rope with a figure-8 knot.

5. If you want to, use heavy-duty metal "S" hooks to shorten your hammock's chains to a comfortable position and to take up the slack when the hammock stretches slightly with use over time.

6. Add extra lengths of heavy-duty chain to the hanging loops if you'll need to adjust the height to accommodate children or smaller adults.

7. Add the pillow, if desired, and climb in.

MAKE A backyard tire swing

Rope (see step 1 to determine length)

A stout tree branch about 12 to 16 feet overhead

Clean, old tire

A piece of rubber hose, approximately the width of your branch (optional; but it will protect both the branch and the rope from wear and tear—see step 3)

Power drill, or awl and hammer

1. To determine the length of rope needed, measure from the tree branch to the point you want the tire to hang, then add approximately ten feet for various loops and knots. (Note: The farther the swing is from the trunk, the larger the supporting branch should be.)

2. Using a figure 8 knot (see How to Tie a Sturdy Knot, page 80), create a loop in the rope about 5 to 8 inches in diameter at one end of the rope. Secure the figure 8 with a stopper knot. Double- and triple-check that this knot is secure.

3. If you can, find a piece of hose with an inside diameter that is slightly larger than the rope, then slip the rope through the hose, and slide it all the way up to the loop. Throw the loop end of the rope over the selected branch. You may need to attach a guide weight to the rope to make for an easier throw—but exercise extreme caution when doing so.

4. Once you have both ends of the rope in your hands, slip the loose end of the rope through the loop in the opposite end. Pull on the loose end of the rope and draw the loop up to the top, securing the rope to the branch.

5. Using the power drill or the awl and hammer, drill or poke several holes through the bottom of the tire. (The holes will keep rainwater from collecting in the tire.)

6. Decide the approximate height you want the tire to hang from, then wrap the rope twice around the tire and use a figure 8 knot secured with a stopper knot to secure the rope at the tire end. You may need to adjust the swing height after a few weeks, as the rope may stretch out from use.

the great **outdoors**

The single best thing about summer is spending time outdoors.

There's more daylight, we all feel healthier, and outdoor activities, as my grandmother would say, help get the blood flowing.

When the temperature rises, it doesn't matter if it's a lake, a pond, a pool, or the ocean—some of us just want to jump in. Water is not only refreshing to splash around in on a hot day, but it makes us more peaceful as well; falling asleep to the sound of the ocean is one of the greatest pleasures. In South Carolina, where we vacation, we spend every moment of sunlight in and on the water. In the mornings we bodysurf and boogie board in the ocean, or kayak on Calibogue Sound, where we're often treated to a visit from a pod of curious dolphin. Later in the day, we take a dip in the pool to cool off before dinner.

But the water isn't the only place to be in the summer months; some of the best moments of my life have been spent on remote trails in the Shawangunk Mountains, the Redwood Forest, or Acadia National Park. In the woods, the day-to-day clatter —car horns, airplane engines, and lawn mowers—is replaced by the peaceful sounds of bird calls, rustling animals, babbling brooks, and rushing waterfalls. Our treks have been rewarded with many magical occurrences—witnessing a newborn baby deer, only minutes old, try to steady himself on wobbly legs; coming within a few feet of a cranky, grumbling black bear; discovering a curious brood of red fox pups who seemed to think we were their parents. In the wood's embrace, events as simple as the sighting of a red-tailed hawk soaring effortlessly overhead can fill one with a sense of joy and wonder.

Closer to home, there's summer in the backyard, passing the hours with old-fashioned lawn games (pages 111–15) like croquet, badminton, and horseshoes. My sister-in-law Arlene, maintains that bocce is the supreme summer game because it leaves a hand free to hold a cocktail. I couldn't agree more.

HOW TO throw and catch a frisbee

The Frisbee legend began in 1871 in Bridgeport, Connecticut, where a man named William Russell Frisbie founded a bakery specializing in homemade pies. Over time, Frisbie's business prospered, and in 1915 he built a new, larger bakery in town. It's said that the bakers would break up their workday by playing catch with the pie tins in a vacant lot. News of the flying Frisbie pie tin game spread to Yale University in nearby New Haven, where it caught on and quickly became a popular on-campus activity.

By the 1940s, the game of Frisbie was so well-known in Connecticut that two enterprising gentlemen, Walter "Fred" Morrison and Warren Franscioni, decided to manufacture a plastic version of the pie tins; they called it the Flyin' Saucer, but the commercial effort failed and the two parted ways. Undaunted, Morrison introduced an improved version in 1957, that he called the Pluto Platter Flying Saucer. Before long Wham-O marketing executives Spud Melin and Dick Knerr licensed the device and christened it the Frisbee in honor of Mr. Frisbie's original pie tins. The Frisbee went on to become one of the most popular toys of all time; over 200 million have been sold since 1957.

throwing directions

1. Holding the Frisbee parallel to the ground, place your thumb on the top of the disc, your index finger on the outside edge of the disc, and curl your pinkie, ring, and middle fingers under the inside edge of the disc.

2. Stand with your feet around shoulder-width apart and your shoulders pointing 90 degrees away from your target.

3. Keeping the disc level, take one step toward your target while simultaneously extending your throwing arm across your body and swinging it away from your body. Release the disc with a snap of the wrist when your arm is about 45 degrees from your body. (You should complete your step and release at approximately the same time.) You may need to practice a few times to get the hang of it.

catching directions

1. Catches can be made with either hand. For low catches, grab the flying disc with your thumb up. For high catches, grab the flying disc with your thumb down.

2. Because the disc is spinning, make sure you squeeze tightly to grab hold.

HOW TO pack for a picnic

Picnics are everything summer should be: informal, peaceful, relaxed. Add a good bottle of wine, a wedge of cheese, and some simple foods, and life doesn't get much better.

tips for making the perfect picnic

» Freeze bottles of water or noncarbonated beverages before you pack them in your picnic basket. Not only will they be nice and cool when you're ready to drink them, but they'll help keep your foods chilled.

» Food spoils quickly in hot weather, so if you're traveling long distances, be sure to carry anything perishable in an ice-filled cooler. If you're driving, transport your picnic basket in the air-conditioned car, not in the steamy trunk.

» Bring foods that are easy to eat, and travel well. Finger foods, hearty sandwiches, and barbecued drumsticks are perfect.

» As simple appetizers, I always bring a few wedges of good cheese, some easy-to-eat fresh fruit (like grapes, cherries, sliced apples or pears), and dried fruit and nuts.

» Use common sense when the temperature soars; in extreme heat, discard any food that's been out of the cooler for more than an hour.

» If you're making sandwiches ahead of time, wrap them in waxed paper so moist ingredients don't get soggy. You might also want to pack sliced tomatoes, roasted red peppers, pickles, and olives separately, so everyone can customize his or her own sandwich.

» Avoid foods with mayonnaise, which can spoil quickly. German potato salad is a good substitute for traditional potato salad because it uses a vinegar-oil dressing.

» Green salads tend to wilt easily, so consider making a vegetable crudité as a side dish instead.

» White wine is a good choice when it's hot, but you may also want to experiment with a fruity rosé, cold champagne with strawberries, or a thermos filled with luscious sangria.

» For dessert, opt for easy-to-handle cookies, brownies, and bars rather than pies or cakes.

don't forget these essentials

» Picnic blanket

» Napkins

» Plates

» Silverware

» Serving utensils

» Condiments (salt, pepper, mustard, roasted red peppers, tapenade)

» Garbage bag

» Radio, or CD player and CDs

» Cups and wine/champagne glasses

» Corkscrew or bottle opener

» Damp wipes

» Insect repellent

» Frisbee

» Candles and flashlight (for evening picnics)

HOW TO protect your skin from the sun

» The sun is strongest from 10 A.M. to 4 P.M., so **stay in the shade** during those hours. Don't be fooled by cloudy or overcast skies—most of the sun's harmful rays can sneak through.

» **Cover up** with clothing, especially a broad-brimmed hat and UV-blocking sunglasses.

» **Wear a broad-spectrum sunscreen** with a sun protection factor (SPF) of 15 or higher. Apply it approximately 30 minutes before going outside; don't forget about hands, ears, feet, shoulders, behind your neck, and hidden places like beneath bathing suit straps that might shift. **Reapply every 2 to 3 hours,** more often if you're really active and sweaty. If you're going to be in the water, use a waterproof sunscreen and reapply it every 2 to 3 hours.

» Lips can get burned, too, so **wear a lip balm with sunscreen.**

» **Use sunscreens on children over the age of six months. Keep newborns out of the sun altogether.**

HOW TO PLAY beach volleyball

Quintessentially Californian, and rightly so, beach volleyball originated in Santa Monica in the 1920s. Today it's played all over the globe, and even became an Olympic sport in 1996. It requires a volleyball net, a volleyball, and at least four players, two per side.

» Scout out a quiet place away from the water and sunbathers, then draw lines in the sand that measure approximately 30 feet wide by 60 feet long.

» The serving player must hit the ball over the net and inside the court lines within three attempts. If the server fails to successfully place the ball within three serves, the opposing team gains control.

» Players rotate positions clockwise whenever their team gains control of the ball. (Thus, each team has a new server at that time.)

» Once the ball is hit over the net to the opposing team, a player cannot contact the ball twice in a row unless the first touch is off a block at the net. A player cannot grab the ball, allow it come to rest in his hand, or touch the net. If he does so, he forfeits the ball to the opposing team.

» A point is earned when the serving team wins a rally, or an ace is served.

» The first team to reach 15 points wins. A match is played in sets of three or five games.

VOLLEYBALL LINGO

ace » A served ball that strikes the opposing team's court in bounds without being touched by a member of the opposing team.

block » Stopping a ball hit by the opposing team before it crosses the net.

bump » Slang for passing the ball.

dig » A difficult, sprawling, close-to-the-ground save.

kill » A powerful hit that the opposing team is unable to return, resulting in a point scored.

match » A set of three or five games. The winner of the two out of three or four out of five games wins the match.

side-out » A mistake by the serving team resulting in a change of serve to the opposing team.

spike » A powerful downward hit of the ball from above the net.

stuff » A dramatic aerial "above the net" block of a spiked ball.

On what was no doubt a steamy July in 1946, the iconic bikini made its debut in Paris. The design was invented and launched almost simultaneously by two Frenchmen, Jacques Heim and Louis Réard. Heim, a swimsuit designer from Cannes, created a two-piece suit that he called the *"Atome"* (French for "atom"). To draw attention to his new creation he hired a skywriter to spell out "Atome—the world's smallest bathing suit" —above the beaches of France. Little did he know that just three weeks later Réard, an engineer, would be unveiling his own daring swimsuit, the "bikini," named after Bikini Atoll in the Pacific Ocean, the site of early atomic bomb testing by the United States. Réard reasoned, rightly, that the bikini, like the bomb, would have an explosive impact on the world. He hired his own plane to skywrite "Bikini—smaller than the smallest bathing suit in the world." Although fashion writers called it scandalous, the style soon took off.

I remember my first bikini perfectly. I was five years old and it was black with pastel polka dots. I'm grateful it's immortalized in a photograph (see the dedication page).

HOW TO DO A flip turn

A flip turn—basically an underwater somersault—is a quick way to change directions when you reach the end of the pool. It looks easy, but will most likely require some practice before you get the hang of it.

1. Swim toward the end of the pool. When you're slightly less than a body length away from the wall, begin to do a forward flip underwater by tucking your chin in toward your chest and rolling your body into a ball. (If you're not wearing nose plugs, make sure you blow air out of your nose so you don't inhale water.)

2. When you're about halfway through your flip, open up your body, extend your legs, and push off against the wall with your feet; you should still be on your back.

3. Streamline your body and roll over onto your stomach as you glide through the water. Keep your shoulders close to your ears, your fingers pointed, and begin kicking.

4. Once your body breaks the surface of the water, start stroking.

HOW TO DO A handstand underwater

Yes, nailing the perfect underwater handstand is possible...even for us grownups! They're easiest in pools, but can be done in lakes too. Once you think you've got it down pat, challenge a friend and see who can hold the pose longest.

1. Go underwater.

2. Start doing a somersault and stop when you can touch the bottom of the pool with your hands. Starting a somersault is as easy as rolling your body forward until your hands graze the bottom of the pool.

3. Put your hands flat on the bottom of the pool and kick your legs up. It's important to keep your arms and legs locked in place and your face pointed straight ahead to keep good balance. Your feet should be locked together with toes pointed upward.

4. To come back up to the surface, push the bottom of the pool with your hands.

WATER SAFETY TIPS FOR KIDS

» Teach children to swim at a young age. It's your best protection in water emergencies.

» Don't rely on "water wings" or flotation devices to keep kids safe in the water. Keeping a watchful eye on them is the most reliable way to ensure their safety.

» Set your own water safety rules for each member of the family based on his or her swimming abilities—for example, young, inexperienced swimmers should stay in waist-deep water.

» Stop swimming at the first sign of a thunderstorm.

» Get certified in cardiopulmonary resuscitation (CPR). Contact the Red Cross or your local fire department for classes nearby. If you have a babysitter, offer to have her/him certified as well.

» Never leave a child unattended in the water or pool area for any reason. If you must leave the pool area, bring the child with you.

» Familiarize yourself with the area; be aware of deep areas, strong currents, or obstructions. Don't allow diving if you are unsure of the depth or conditions beneath the surface.

» Make sure your kids know how important it is to follow the lifeguard's instructions. Point out the nearest lifeguard stand when you first arrive at the beach or pool.

» At the beach, find a landmark near where you're sitting and show your children. This is a great way for them to know how to find you if they wander off.

» A child should swim with a buddy so that each can watch out for the other and make sure safe behavior is being observed.

BEACH CRUISERS

One of the great joys of the season is untethering yourself from four-wheeled, gas-guzzling vehicles and replacing them with two knobby tires powered by two underutilized legs. Beach bikes and cruisers, with their fat, gripy tires are well saved for getting you through thick, wet sand. they're usually one speed and have coaster brakes. If you're looking for the classic bike of yesteryear for cruising around town consider a "Townie." Townies are more upright than beach bikes, have thinner tires, three speeds, and a basket upfront for stowing Toto..

We practically live on our beach bikes from June to September. We track the tide and plan our biking adventures accordingly, since the last thing you want—and believe me, we've learned this from experience—is to find yourself caught three miles down the beach with a rising tide between you and home. As a rule, you should head out an hour or two before low tide, allowing plenty of time to ride before the ocean shifts again. Along the way we stop to refuel with a basket of salty tortilla chips and a heaping bowl of guacamole from the cantina down the beach, and wash it all down with a puckery margarita or two.

BIKE DEALERS

If you're interested in purchasing a beach bike or a "Townie" for jaunts around town, below are a few manufacturers that are worth looking into. Check local listings or directions for rentals.

Electra Bicycle Company
2262 Rutherford Road, Suite 104
Carlsbad, CA 92008
Tel: 1-760-607-2453
www.electrabike.com
With wild paint styles and fun names like the Rockabilly, the Rat Fink, the Suzy Q, and the Hawaii, Electra epitomizes beach bike cool.

Schwinn
Tel: 1-800-SCHWINN
www.schwinnbike.com
In business since 1895, Schwinn is an American icon. Schwinn's classic Cruiser, first designed in 1955, is the undisputed granddaddy of the beach bike. Schwinn also sells a neat tandem (built for two) Cruiser.

Nirve Sports Limited
18401 Bandilier Circle
Fountain Valley, CA 92708
Tel.: 1-888-BY-NIRVE
www.nirve.com
Nirve has some excellent beach bikes, including a Chopper series that motorcycle lovers will adore.

HOW TO RIDE A boogie board

Short, wide, and made of light foam core, a boogie board is similar to a surfboard, except that it's ridden lying down. While they're not a must, wearing swim fins or flippers will increase your speed significantly.

1. Paddle out to beyond the break and wait for a great wave. As it approaches, lie face down on the board and direct it toward shore. Grab the front of the board with both hands and begin to kick hard to catch the wave before it breaks.

2. Once you catch a wave, you can move left or right. To go left, pull up on the right rail (the outside edge of the boogie board) and keep your left hand on the front. To head right, do the reverse.

3. As you gain momentum, pull your body forward, arch your back, and lift your head high. To remain on the wave's face, pull up on the outside rail, causing the wave-side edge of the board to dig into the face. Alternately, release the outside rail to slide down the wave's face.

4. To gain speed, keep your feet up and out of the water. To slow down, drag them through the water.

HOW TO BODY SURF

Bodysurfing is simply a way to ride the waves to shore without the assistance of a buoyant item, such as a boogie board or surfboard. While it can definitely be done without swim fins or flippers, it's easier and much more fun to surf with them.

» Swim out past the break and wait for a great wave.

» When one approaches, begin swimming in the same direction to catch it before it breaks.

» As you begin to move with the wave, swim left or right for the longest ride, straight ahead for the most speed.

» As you gain momentum, kick your feet, but stop stroking your arms, then extend one arm forward (your right arm to go right, left to go left), with your palm facing downward just breaking the surface of the water; streamline your body and ride the wave as long as you can.

3 WAYS TO BECOME A BETTER SWIMMER

» Using flippers or swim fins makes it easier to hold a better body position, which in turn allows you to focus on other parts of your technique, such as body roll or timing.

» Slow down. It may be frustrating, but if you try to go fast with bad technique you're wasting energy. Get your technique down first, then introduce speed.

» Have a friend videotape you swimming, then watch it back at home and look for where your stroke or body positioning might be causing water drag. Seeing your mistakes will probably help you improve at least one facet of your stroke.

HOW TO fly a kite

It's believed that kites made their appearance in China more than three thousand years ago. The frame was made of bamboo, the sail and bridle of silk. Today they're constructed of lightweight wood and either silk, nylon, paper, or plastic. While there are many types of kites, the most common are the sled, the winged box, the delta, the box, and the classic diamond.

» Before heading out, check to see if local weather conditions are favorable. Generally a wind speed of 5 to 15 mph is best.

» Look for a large, open space free of trees, buildings, and power lines.

» There are two ways to launch a kite. The first is to hold it in both hands, making sure you hold the spool of string as well, then toss it gently into the air so that the wind will catch it and lift it up. (You may have to try a few times). The second is to let out a small length of string and begin running with the kite behind you until the wind lifts it into the air.

» Once the kite is aloft, begin letting out more string until the kite reaches a desired height (normal heights range from 50 to 100 feet). If it dips, simply run a short distance in the opposite direction or pull in the string a bit to give it some lift.

» When you're ready to bring the kite in, slowly wind the string around the spool. When it's within reach, grab it before it hits the ground to avoid damaging it.

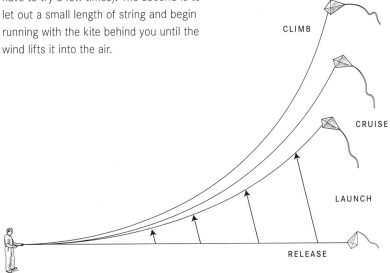

CLIMB

CRUISE

LAUNCH

RELEASE

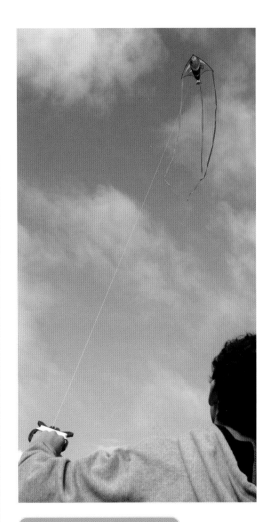

The highest recorded altitude a single kite has reached is 12,471 feet—that's over 2 miles.

One year we packed little more than our swimsuits, some flip-flops, and a well-worn collection of reggae CDs, and headed to Jamaica for a much-needed long holiday. At the end of an active day, we'd be near starving, but our cook, Auntie Hanna, would make us wait until sunset before serving dinner. She'd swat us out of her kitchen like children, consoling us with a small plate of fritters made from callaloo or saltfish, and two icy Red Stripe beers to carry down to the shore. While Bob Marley, Peter Tosh, or Jimmy Cliff serenaded us from the stereo inside, we'd sit back in awe as the sky turned the most extraordinary shades of marmalade, guava, and spun sugar.

Reggae, the music of Jamaica, is the music of summer. An intoxicating fusion of the beats of Kingston and American rhythm and blues, and a symbol of both liberation and relaxation, reggae conjures images of rum-spiked drinks, palm trees, clear blue waters, and sun-kissed skin. Essential listening during the carefree days of summer, reggae is the perfect antidote to those cold, gray winter days when summer seems so far away.

JERRY'S TOP 5 REGGAE CDS

If the weather is warm and the sun is shining, you can bet that Jerry is speeding around town in his Mini Cooper with the roof open and reggae blasting. These are his picks for must-have summer reggae albums.

1. *Legend*, Bob Marley
2. *Reggae Vibrations*, Various Artists
3. *Jamaica*, Various Artists
4. *Equal Rights*, Peter Tosh
5. *The Harder They Come*, Jimmy Cliff

SURFING

Are you a Bitchen Betty or a Chubby Checker? Do you know the difference between a shubie and a switchfoot? Are you a wacko, or a waxboy? Surf fanatics have their own unique language and culture, all of which originated in the Hawaiian and Southern California surf scenes.

Originally developed by Hawaiian islanders, *he'e nalu* ("wave sliding") spread to the continental United States in the early twentieth century. Surfers used heavy timber boards to ride the swells; it wasn't until the 1950s and 1960s, when less expensive, more maneuverable, and lighter boards made of fiberglass and foam became available, that the sun-stoked surfer culture truly began. Today the sport is embraced by sunnies all around the globe; we ride sticks, drive sandboxes, and yearn for tunnel love. For those of you Barneys out there who need a little help, we provide a short guide to surfer slang.

HOW TO USE A skim board

Skim boarding, or "sand skimming," resembles surfing in that you ride on the water while standing on a board. The similarity ends there: while surfing is done in deep water, skim boarding is done on the shoreline, in less than an inch of water. The boards vary in size and composition, but most are made of laminated wood and are oval- or teardrop-shaped.

1. Scout out a good location. The ideal spot for sand skimming is a beach with a slight slope, preferably away from crowds since you'll be skimming along the shoreline.

2. Watch the pattern of the waves and start when the most recent wave is just beginning to head back out. When the water from the retreating wave becomes very shallow (around ½ to 1 inch), place one hand on each edge of your board and start running along the beach, headed slightly toward the water.

3. Throw the board down flat into the shallow water; it should skim across the surface. Gently place one foot on the tail of the board first, then swing your opposite foot forward and place it in the middle-front of the board. Don't jump or hop on—you'll definitely fall! Bend your knees slightly and extend your hands for balance.

4. By gradually shifting your weight onto the board, you'll be able to maintain speed and move forward smoothly. Continue skimming until the board comes to a stop.

SURF SLANG

babelini » A pretty girl.

barney » A newbie; beginner.

betty » A girl who surfs.

bitchen » Cool; awesome.

chubby checker » A poser.

maytagged » Wiping out.

sandbox » An old VW van with a bunch of surfboards on the roof.

shubie » Somebody who wears or buys surf gear but has never actually surfed.

stick » A surfboard.

stoked » Wild with enthusiasm.

sunnies » People who stay in the sun all the time and have great tans.

switchfoot » Someone who can surf with either foot forward.

tunnel love » To hang in a tube for more than ten seconds.

wacko » A daredevil.

waxboy » Someone who sits on the beach waxing his board but never actually hits the water.

7 MOVIES TO GET YOU IN THE SURFING SPIRIT

» *Gidget* (1959)
» *Blue Hawaii* (1961)
» *The Endless Summer* (1966)
» *Big Wednesday* (1978)
» *Point Break* (1991)
» *Step into Liquid* (2003)
» *Riding Giants* (2004)

Like fine wines, aged cheeses, and most women, some cars get better with age. I'm talking about rugged, fun-loving cars that weather well and come alive during wind-in-your-hair drives along backcountry lanes, sandy beach roads, and winding mountain trails. Cars like the International Scout, the Volkswagen Thing, the Jeep Scrambler, and the classic Ford Woody.

The Woody is perhaps the most iconic car of summer. These wood-bodied station wagons were the SUVs of their day and became the transportation of choice for sixties surfers who needed large vehicles to haul their boards. The name made its way from the Southern California surfing scene into mainstream vocabulary through songs like "Surf City" by Jan and Dean, which perfectly captures the spirit of the summer jalopy:

> *I bought a '30 Ford wagon and we call it a woody.*
> *Surf City, here we come.*
> *You know it's not very cherry, it's an oldie but a goodie.*
> *Surf City, here we come.*
> *Well, it ain't got a back seat or a rear window,*
> *but it still gets me where I wanna go.*

I don't own a Woody, but I do own a well-worn Jeep Wrangler that's festooned with stickers from places like the Surf Shack in Bodega Bay, the Black Dog on Martha's Vineyard, and the Gilded Otter in New Paltz, New York. It has a soft-top roof that leaks when it rains, and the floorboards are getting thin in places, but when I drive it with the top down on a summer's day, I wouldn't trade it for anything in the world.

THE BEACH TOWEL

With its sunny colors and cheery patterns, an oversized beach towel not only lifts your spirits but serves a multitude of uses as well. Easily accommodating even the largest adult after a chilly ocean swim, it can be used as a private changing room for slipping out of sandy swimsuits, or as a cozy "tent" for napping. When I got tired of scrunching one up to use as a headrest, I cut up a few and used them to cover small pillows. They're perfect for around the pool—they look summery and fun, and the terry cloth is soft and comfortable on a hot day.

HOW TO MAKE A beach towel pillow

Both decorative and useful, these brightly patterned pillows can be made in under an hour, and they look great both indoors and out.

Large beach towel

One 12- to 18-inch square pillow insert
(consider recycling old, worn-out throw pillows)

Tape measure

Sewing machine

Thread

Straight pins

Scissors

1. Determine the measurements of the pillow by measuring from edge to edge with the tape measure. Open the beach towel and place it face up on a flat surface.

2. You will need to cut the towel into three sections: one piece to cover the front, and two smaller pieces that will make up the back. For the front piece (starting at one end of the towel), measure, then cut the fabric so it is 4 inches larger than the size of your pillow. For example, if your pillow is 12 inches square, your fabric should measure 16 x 16 inches. If your pillow is 18 inches square, your fabric should measure 22 x 22 inches.

3. Cut the fabric for the back of the pillow. Starting from the end again, measure, then cut the fabric, so that it measures four inches larger than the pillow from top to bottom, and eight inches longer from side to side. For instance, if your pillow is 18 inches square, your fabric should be 22 x 26 inches. Make sure you cut the fabric so that the pattern will line up evenly on the seams. Find the middle of the fabric by either measuring with your tape measure or folding it in half; cut along that line to make two pieces. You should now have three pieces of fabric. Discard the leftover beach towel fabric.

4. Line up the three pieces of fabric end to end, face down on the work surface, with the larger piece in the center. Be sure to line up the patterns between the three pieces. Using straight pins, pin the side of one back panel to the front panel, good sides facing, allowing for a 1½" seam. Repeat on the other side of the front panel, using the remaining back panel. With your sewing machine, carefully sew the three sections together on the inside. Remove the pins. You should now have one long piece of fabric.

5. Finish the ends of the towel. With the fabric facing down, fold the left edge in 1" and pin, then do the same on the right side. Sew those hems closed and remove the pins.

6. You are now ready to finish your pillow. Place the fabric face up on your work surface and fold the left side in at the seam. Next, fold the right side in at the seam. You should be looking at the inside of the fabric. Pin across the top of the folded fabric to create a 1½" seam, then do the same at the bottom. Using the sewing machine, sew the top and bottom seams.

7. Turn the pillowcase inside out, so the outer fabric is facing you, and insert pillow through the back flap.

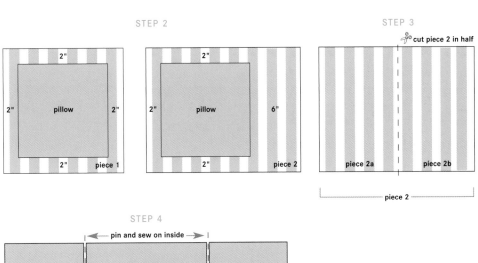

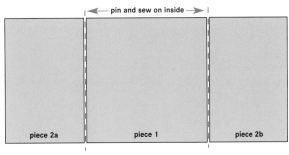

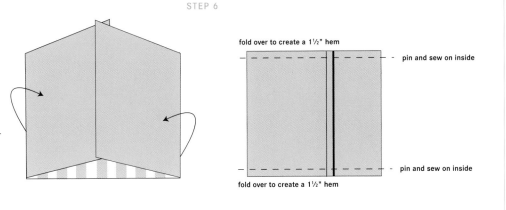

HOW TO MAKE A sarong

You can buy a sarong in a store and look like everyone else at the pool, or you can easily make your own and look fabulously unique. Hem all four edges of a rectangular piece of cotton, silk, or sheer fabric four to five yards long and a yard wide and voilà—you're finished. When you're ready to head to the café for lunch, just put one on and go. Try layering them for a bright, colorful look.

1. Wrap the fabric around your waist and grab a corner in each hand.

2. Knot the corners together twice, so they're secure, then adjust the ends so that the knot looks good.

3. Rotate the sarong so the knot sits above one of your hips. You can leave the tie out or tuck the ends in.

STEP 2

STEP 1

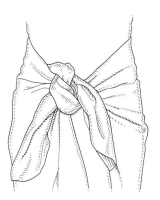

STEP 3

BEACH ESSENTIALS

» Waterproof sunscreen

» Sunglasses

» Hats

» Extra clothes (don't forget sweatshirts for later in the day)

» Umbrella

» Beach blanket

» Towels

» Folding chairs

» Goggles

» Water and sand toys

» Magazines/paperback book

» Cooler/snacks

» Moist towelettes

» Bottled water

» Large Ziploc bags (to collect seashells and store wet swimsuits on the way home)

HOW TO build a sand castle

Shell-encrusted turrets, hand-dug moats, driftwood drawbridges—sand architects know how satisfying it can be to construct a dramatic castle on a long stretch of white beach.

» To get started, you'll need a few tools—plastic pails and shovels, cups, spoons, dull knives, melon ballers, garden trowels, and putty knives. A long-handled shovel may come in handy to move large quantities of sand.

» Choose a building spot that's not too close to the water's edge, but not so far from the surf that the sand will be too dry to work with.

» Dig down until you hit wet sand. Remove the wet sand and place it in a mound on the beach—this will form the base of your castle, so make sure there's enough to start sculpting.

» The secret to building a sturdy sand castle is to start at the top of the pile of wet sand and work downward, so the drying sand won't roll off and mar your efforts. Move steadily, carving off a bit at a time.

» Gently add wet sand in layers to create towers and spires. Form a handful of wet sand into bricks and arrange them into walls.

» To add a "dark forest," create trees by slowly squeezing handfuls of very wet sand into loose towers. As you work, your dream castle will begin to emerge. But don't get too attached to your masterpiece—high tide will roll in soon enough.

RESOURCES

» Read *Sandcastles Made Simple* by Lucinda Wierenga (Stewart, Tabori & Chang, 2005).

» Can't get to the beach? Bake a sand castle instead. Try the sand-castle-shaped Bundt pan from NordicWare. Visit www.nordicware.com.

BOATING

It was on Uncle Sy's boat, the *Nauti Lady,* that I got my sea legs at age seven. To my brothers and me, an invitation to spend a day on the *Nauti Lady* was the equivalent of winning the lottery. We would head to the marina on a clear Saturday morning and set sail for Long Island Sound, calling out as loud as we could "The *Nauti Lady* rides again!" as we passed under the Throgs Neck Bridge. We'd drop anchor in a quiet cove, where we'd spend hours swimming and clamming in the briny waters until our fingers were puckered like raisins. Back on board, we'd shuck our clams in the galley and serve them up with lemon wedges and a spicy-hot cocktail sauce.

My uncle, who loved his boat only slightly less than he loved his wife, taught us how to tie intricate nautical knots like the figure 8 and the sailor's knot. At sunset, we'd head back to the marina, where the party would spill out of the adjacent boats onto the docks and continue well past our bedtimes. Exhausted from the day's activities, we'd inevitably fall asleep during the car ride back home.

HOW TO tie a sturdy knot

My uncle Sy taught me how to tie these nautical knots when I was a child, and thirty years later, I find myself still using them in my day-to-day life. Knowing how to tie a practical knot is invaluable when you're hitching an anchor, making a rope swing, pitching a tent, or simply stringing up a hammock in the backyard.

FIGURE 8 KNOT

SQUARE KNOT

SAILOR'S KNOT

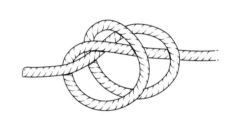

STOPPER KNOT

DOUBLE HALF-HITCH KNOT

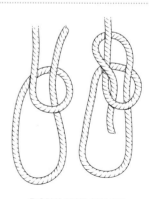

BOWLINE KNOT

GETTING NAUTY: NAUTICAL TERMS FOR NOVICES

Stumped as to whether you're heading windward or leeward? This handy lexicon will have you sounding like a sailor in no time at all.

abaft » Toward the rear (stern) of the ship.

aft » Toward the stern of the ship.

aground » Touching or resting on the ground or bottom.

alee » Away from the direction of the wind; the opposite of windward.

aloft » Above deck.

aweigh » The position of an anchor just clear of the bottom.

batten down » To secure hatches and loose objects in the hull and on deck.

bilge » The interior of the hull below the floor boards.

bitter end » The last part of a rope or cable.

bow » The front part of a ship.

bulkhead » An upright partition that separates compartments.

cabin » The living compartment for passengers.

draft » The depth of a ship's keel below the waterline.

fathom » A unit of length that equals six feet.

fluke » The wedge-shaped part of an anchor that digs into the bottom.

fore » Toward the front part (bow) of the ship.

galley » The kitchen area.

head » The toilet.

helm » The wheel or tiller that steers the ship.

hold » A compartment below deck used for carrying cargo.

hull » The main body of a boat.

keel » The centerline of a ship running fore and aft.

knot » A measure of speed equal to one nautical mile (6,076 feet) per hour.

lee side » The side of the ship that is sheltered from the wind.

leeward » In the direction that the wind is blowing toward; opposite of windward.

mainmast » The tallest mast.

mast » A vertical pole that supports sails or rigging.

nautical mile » A nautical unit of length that equals approximately 6,076 feet.

port » The left side of a ship looking forward. Also means harbor.

rudder » The vertical blade that helps steer the ship.

scuppers » Drain holes that allow water to run off the deck.

starboard » The right side of a ship facing forward.

stem » The forward most part of the bow.

stern » The rear part of the ship.

topsail » The second sail (from the bottom) up a mast.

windward » In the direction the wind is coming from; opposite of leeward.

HOW TO paddle a canoe

Thousands of years ago, Native Americans used large tree trunks, which they shaped and hollowed, to travel across water. Later, a more practical version evolved with a frame, of wooden ribs, that was covered with white birch bark—not only lightweight and smooth, but waterproof and resilient as well.

1. If you're canoeing with a partner, sit or kneel in the canoe facing forward at either the stern or the bow of the canoe. If you're canoeing alone, sit or kneel in the middle.

2. Hold the paddle by placing your "inside" hand toward the top and your "waterside" hand in a comfortable spot approximately 2 to 3 feet farther down the handle of the paddle. Your knuckles should be facing away from your body.

3. Place the paddle blade in the water as far forward as you can reach without bending or lunging forward (approximately 2 feet for an adult), and at the same time push your top hand forward and pull your bottom hand back, drawing the paddle blade through the water, while making sure to keep the top of the paddle handle below eye level.

4. Pivot your shoulders to draw the blade straight back through the water until it's approximately even with your hip (but no farther, as that will slow down the canoe), then lift the blade out of the water and rotate it so it is parallel to the surface of the water. Smoothly swing the paddle back to the starting position, place the blade back into the water, and continue to stroke.

5. To paddle backward, while sitting or kneeling in your canoe, rotate your shoulders 90 degrees toward your paddling side and look over your shoulder to the back of the canoe. Hold your paddle normally, and insert the blade into water approximately 1 to 2 feet behind you. Push forward with your top hand and pull backward with your bottom hand, drawing the blade of the paddle toward the front of the boat. The canoe should begin to move backward.

CAN U CANOE?

» Always enter low. The lower your center of gravity, the more stable your canoe will be. When you're getting on, off, or changing positions, make sure to stay low and keep one hand on the side rail, or gunwale.

» Don't overload! Know the maximum load capacity for your canoe and respect it.

» With two people, you'll usually want to paddle on opposite sides of the canoe. The person sitting in the rear (the stern) is responsible for steering and the person up front in the bow provides the power strokes.

» Canoes should never be stored directly on a concrete or earthen floor. Resting canoes bottomside up will add years to their life span.

HOW TO get up on water skis

Learning to water-ski is sort of like learning to roller skate—you may fall down the first few times, but it doesn't take long to get the hang of it. While it may look easier to start off of a dock, it's not; beginners should learn to water-ski from the water. And always remember that the secret to waterskiing is to relax and let the boat do the work!

» While wearing your life vest and skis, grab on to the rope handle with both hands (keeping your arms slightly bent), and place it between your knees. Position yourself about 15 feet behind the boat, facing forward.

» Crouch in the water, with your knees drawn up near your chest, and the tips of your skis facing up. When you are ready, signal the boat pilot by calling out "okay," or nodding your head.

» As the boat starts to move forward, lean back slightly, keeping your knees bent as if you were sitting in a chair. Don't pull on the rope, or rush to stand up—just let the boat pull you into position. (A common mistake that beginners make is leaning too far forward or too far backward, so try to keep your feet parallel, and directly under you, about 1–2½ feet apart from each other.)

» Stay in the crouched position as the boat gains speed, then begin to straighten your arms as you stand up, leaning slightly back. Once you are up and skiing, try to keep your knees bent to absorb the bumps. And, most important, relax!

» When you're done, let go of the rope in deep water; you will ski for another 40 or so feet before sinking down.

WATERSKIING SIGNALS

» A thumbs-up signal means go faster

» A thumbs-down signal means go slower.

» A hand flat, palm down, moving back and forth motion means stay at this speed.

» A slicing motion at your neck means "Kill the motor!"

HOW TO **track the tides**

Anyone who has ever spent time by the ocean knows that tracking the ebb and flow of the tides is important when planning water-related activities. We learned our lesson a few years back, when we embarked on a long kayak trip during the new moon. Not realizing the dramatic tidal impact these spring tides have, we were shocked to discover that there was not enough water left in the channel at low tide for us to get back to shore. Tired, hungry, and, in my case, cranky, we were forced to paddle around Calibogue Sound until the tide eventually turned in our favor.

what is a tide?

The word *tides* is a generic term used to define the alternating rise and fall in sea level with respect to the land (tides also occur in large lakes, the atmosphere, and even within the crust of the earth, but to a much smaller degree). Tides are created because the Earth and the moon (imagine them being like magnets) are attracted to each other. As the moon tugs at the Earth to bring it closer, water—because it is fluid and always moving—is affected by the pull.

how to track them

Each day, there are two high tides and two low tides (the ocean is in constant movement from high tide to low tide, back to high tide again). There are slightly less than 12½ hours between the two high tides, so if you don't have a tide chart handy (these are often found in your local newspaper), you can easily do the math to find out when it will be high again, or low. For example, if high tide is at 9:00 A.M. on Monday morning, simply add 12 hours and 24 minutes to that time, and you can estimate that it will be high again at around 9:24 P.M. on Monday evening, then again at 9:48 A.M. on Tuesday morning. To determine when it will be low, simply add 6 hours and 12 minutes to the high tide time; if the tide is high at 9:00 A.M., for example, it will be low at about 3:12 P.M.

types of tides

SPRING TIDES

Despite their name, spring tides have nothing to do with the season; they occur when the moon is full or new, and the gravitational pull of the moon and sun are combined, resulting in extreme tide levels (about 20 percent higher or lower than average).

NEAP TIDES

Neap tides are especially weak tides that occur twice a month, during the moon's quarter phases, when the gravitational forces of the moon and the sun are perpendicular to one another, with respect to the Earth.

THE PROXIGEAN SPRING TIDE

The Proxigean spring tide is a rare, unusually high tide that happens, at most, every 1½ years. This very high tide, well-known for causing extreme flooding and coastal erosion, occurs when the moon is both unusually close to the Earth and in the new moon phase.

HOW TO take a day hike

The number one rule for hiking? New socks, old shoes. While a brand new pair of boots looks great, you definitely don't want to discover that they're blister-makers miles down the trail. Thoroughly break in a new pair by using them regularly around the house and yard before embarking on a strenuous hike. I recommend a midweight boot with an all-leather upper; a waterproof lining will ensure that your feet are dry and comfortable even in the wettest weather.

day hike essentials

I've done a lot of hiking over the years, and I've learned plenty from my mistakes; I've been lost without a compass, baked in the sun without sunscreen or lip balm, gotten miserable blisters without having a Band-Aid handy. While this may seem like a lot to carry for a day in the woods, everything on the list easily fits into a backpack.

» Sweatshirt/jacket (quick-drying synthetic materials are best)

» Local trail maps/ guidebooks (study them and plan your route before setting out)

» Compass

» Whistle

» Insect repellent

» Water

» Hat

» Pocketknife

» Tissues/Wet-Ones

» Wristwatch

» Snacks/trail mix

» Sunglasses

» Sunscreen

» Lip balm

» Extra socks

» Band-Aids

» Cell phone

» Money

» Identification

» Small mirror

» Bandana

» Waterproof matches or lighter

» Large garbage bag

HOW TO USE A CRICKET AS A THERMOMETER

If there are crickets nearby, you can measure the air temperature by listening to their chirping and applying this simple formula:

1. Count the number of times a cricket chirps in 14 seconds.

2. Add 40 to this number. The resulting number is approximately the air temperature in degrees Fahrenheit.

the amazing garbage bag

It's hard to imagine ever actually looking forward to wearing a garbage bag, but when you're three miles from shelter and an unexpected rainstorm hits, believe me—you'll happily throw one on.

» If you're caught in a downpour, cut an opening in the middle of the closed end and pull it over your body for an instant rain poncho.

» To make a survival blanket (hypothermia can occur in 50°F. weather), pack it with leaves or pine needles and cover your body with it.

when is a bandana not a bandana?

In a pinch, a bandana can be used as a water strainer, a signal flag, a potholder, a lashing material, a sling, a washcloth, and even as kindling to start a fire.

my 8 rules for safe hiking

1 Proper planning is essential (see the checklist opposite). Check the weather conditions and refer to trail maps and guidebooks to get a sense of the trail distance, estimated time, and difficulty level before you set out. Keep in mind that a fit hiker will tend to average about two miles per hour on the trail.

2 Never hike alone.

3 Make sure that people back home are aware of your itinerary and expected return time. Don't forget to check in with them when you get back.

4 Start early so that you have plenty of time to finish your hike well before dark.

5 Mark your progress on your map so you know where you are at all times.

6 Drink plenty of water. Stay away from soda and alcohol as they tend to dehydrate you. Unless absolutely necessary, don't drink from streams or lakes.

7 Never approach or attempt to feed wild animals. In most cases, the animals are more afraid of you than you are of them. If you encounter a snake, don't make any sudden movements as it may strike; simply stay calm and slowly move away.

8 If you're in trouble, use your whistle. Three short whistles mean you need assistance.

IF YOU'RE LOST

» Use your cell phone if you can get a signal.

» Although it may be difficult, remaining calm and composed is essential to survival in an emergency. The first thing you need to do is assess your situation and formulate a plan; your priorities should be shelter, water, fire, and rest/sleep. The human body can survive for days or even weeks without food, but not long without water, so make hydration your priority.

» If you have a small mirror, flash the universal Morse code signal for SOS: three short, three long, and three short signals. Pause. Repeat the signal. You can also use a camera flash, a flashlight, or aluminum foil to signal for help, or blow your whistle. If there's a large clearing, try spelling out SOS with rocks and/or logs.

» Stay dry to prevent hypothermia. Build a lean-to (page 89) as a shelter and, if you have matches, a campfire. To help start a fire, gather dead twigs and sap from evergreen trees since the resins ignite quickly.

my favorite trail mix

My husband teases me that dried cranberries give me super powers when we're out hiking. I think it's true—this trail mix will give you the energy you need to make it through the last two miles.

- 2 cups dried cranberries
- 1 cup raisins
- 1 cup natural almonds
- 1 cup natural cashews
- 1 cup unsalted pepita seeds
- 6 ounces mixed dried fruit bits

Mix together the ingredients. Stored in an airtight container, it will keep for several weeks. » makes approximately 7 cups

GORP is a common name for trail mix. It stands for Good Old Raisins and Peanuts.

HOW TO build a campfire

Guaranteed to warm body and soul. Make sure campfires are legal where you are.

- Kindling (sticks, small logs from fallen branches, dry leaves, paper) and logs
- Bucket of water, or water source
- Shovel
- Small- to medium-sized rocks and stones (for optional fire ring)

1. Build your fire at least 10 feet away from tents, trees, roots, and other flammable items. A fire ring is simple to build with stones and rocks and helps contain the fire. If you can't build one, just clear a space 24 to 32 inches across.

2. Gather dry firewood and kindling, using only fallen branches, then build a small, loose pile of twigs, dry leaves, paper, and kindling, allowing space for air to flow through and feed the fire.

3. Build a pyramid of dry twigs and small sticks around and above the pile of kindling, allowing space for the air to flow through and feed the fire. Light the kindling with a match.

4. As the fire grows in strength, add increasingly larger sticks, then logs, making sure to always leave enough space between them for the fire to breathe.

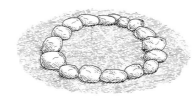

STEP 1

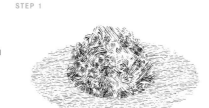

STEP 2

STEP 3

STEP 4

CONSCIENTIOUS CAMPING

Here are some environmentally friendly products to take on your next camping trip. They're also good to use in your outdoor shower, or even in the lake.

» No-Rinse Shampoo—the perfect way to keep your hair clean when water is in short supply. Plus it's biodegradable.

» Stearns Sun Shower—this easy-to-pack, solar-powered product lets you enjoy a hot shower anytime, anywhere.

» Campsuds Soap—an all-purpose, biodegradable soap that works in hot, cold, and salt water. You can use it on dishes and your hair! Also available in a citronella scent, which helps repel insects.

» Dr. Bronner's—this classic can be used for everything from bathing to mouthwash.

» Many brands make eco-friendly products, so if you aren't doing such serious camping, they're probably all you need: Aveda, Burt's Bees, Jason Natural, Kiss My Face, and Tom's of Maine.

CAMPFIRE SAFETY TIPS

building and burning

» Build a fire only as big as you need.

» Never build a fire near tents or other flammable items.

» Never use flammable fluids to start a fire.

» Never leave fire unattended.

» Keep a bucket of water and a shovel nearby just in case.

afterward

» Make sure to completely extinguish the fire when you're done.

» Scatter the ashes or embers, then sprinkle with water. Stir with a stick. Repeat.

» Drench the charred logs.

» Repeat until everything is cold.

HOW TO build a lean-to

If you're lost in the woods and need to hunker down for the night or ride out a storm, you can stay warm and protected by crafting this simple lean-to out of logs, branches, and leaves. In an ideal world, it would be built next to a small cave, or a rock overhang into which you could snuggle for protection. If you can't find a cave or overhang, try to build your structure against a fallen tree or a large rock.

» If possible, select a spot at least 50 yards from a body of water (the water will add dampness to the air) and away from your campfire, so it can't catch fire. Scour the area for building materials, including fallen branches, twigs, leaves, and moss—anything that will add insulation and strength.

» Lean sturdy sticks and branches up against your support structure. Leave enough room to sleep under, but not so much that you'll lose body heat.

» Pile smaller branches, leaves, twigs, and moss on top of the frame to insulate and weatherproof it, leaving an exposed opening at either end so you can move in and out.

AVOIDING LIGHTNING IN THE WILDERNESS

» Always monitor the sky for changes in weather conditions that signal a storm. At the first sound of thunder—or earlier, if the sky has grown dark—leave exposed areas such as fields, beach areas, and mountain peaks.

» If you're caught in a storm, your first priority should be protection. Lightning is attracted to water, so head away from beaches or lakes. It also seeks out the tallest objects, so stay as low as possible. Head toward uniform cover, such as a wooded area, but avoid solitary trees, small trenches, and caves. (There may be metals in the rocks, which will attract lightning.)

» If you're in a group, it's best to spread out 50 to 100 feet apart to minimize the risk of multiple injuries.

» Remove any metal jewelry.

» Lightning that strikes an object on the ground can travel, so find something to insulate you from the ground, such as a sleeping bag, backpack (metal frame facing down), or sweatshirt. Place your feet on the object and try to make your body as small as possible by rolling yourself into a ball and covering your head with your arms.

> To estimate how many miles away a storm is, count the number of seconds that elapse between a flash of lightning and its corresponding bang of thunder, then divide that number by five.

if someone is struck

» A lightning strike can cause severe damage to the body and may even be fatal. If someone in your party has been struck by lightning, call 911 immediately for assistance. If their heartbeat or breathing has stopped, administer CPR or mouth-to-mouth resuscitation.

» If you are still in an active thunderstorm and continue to be at risk for a strike, consider moving the victim and yourself to a safer location.

identifying common leaves

BLACK SPRUCE

EASTERN WHITE PINE

BALSAM FIR

WHITE OAK

AMERICAN ELM

AMERICAN BEECH

SUGAR MAPLE

AMERICAN MOUNTAIN ASH

PAPER BIRCH

DATE PALM

COCONUT PALM

identifying clouds

STRATUS

Stratus clouds are horizontal, layered clouds that usually cover the entire sky. They vary in color from dark gray to nearly white and produce only a light mist or drizzle.

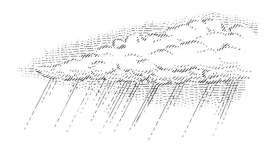

NIMBOSTRATUS

These low-altitude clouds form a dark gray layer and produce light to moderate precipitation. When they grow vertically, it means a thunderstorm could develop quickly.

CUMULUS

Cumulus clouds are fair weather clouds that look like puffy balls of cotton floating in the sky. They are usually isolated, with large areas of blue sky in between them.

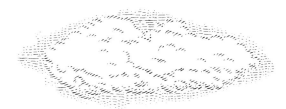

STRATOCUMULUS

This low, lumpy layer of clouds is gray, white, or a mixture of both, with dark patches. These clouds bring no precipitation, but are often seen at the beginning or end of a storm.

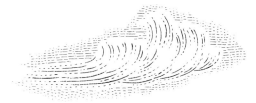

CIRRUS

These are very high, thin, wispy clouds that sunlight can pass through. They occur in fair weather but are sometimes a sign of an approaching frontal system or the remnants of a thunderstorm.

identifying animal tracks

BLACK BEAR

front foot
4 1/2"

hind foot
7"-9"

BOBCAT

front foot
2"

hind foot
2"

COTTONTAIL RABBIT

front foot
1"

hind foot
4"

COYOTE

front foot
2 1/2"

hind foot
2 1/4"

GRAY SQUIRREL

front foot
1 1/2"

hind foot
2 1/4"

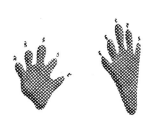

MOOSE

4 1/2"-5 1/2"

OPOSSUM

front foot
1 3/4"

hind foot
2"

PORCUPINE

front foot
2 1/2"

hind foot
3"

RACCOON

front foot
2 1/2"

hind foot
4"

RED FOX

front foot
2 1/4"

hind foot
2"

STRIPED SKUNK

front foot
1 1/4"

hind foot
2"

TURKEY

4"

WHITE-TAILED DEER

2 1/2"-3"

WOLF

front foot
4 1/4"-4 3/4"

hind foot
4 1/4"-4 3/4"

WOODCHUCK

front foot
2"

hind foot
2 1/4"

One of the highlights of my family's annual New England clambake (see page 144) is building a campfire just before sunset. It's a natural place for friends and family to reconnect and catch up on the events of the previous year. In accordance with tradition, around nine o'clock someone will produce a bag of marshmallows and the more ambitious of the group will scout around for long toasting sticks. As the marshmallows are held over the fire, we tend to debate the ideal point of marshmallow "doneness." Camps are formed between those who prefer a dark, crispy shell with a gooey, lavalike interior, and those who favor a toasted golden-brown body with a warm, pliant texture. In any event, when the marshmallows are ready, we patiently blow on them until they're cool enough to eat, or sandwich them between two graham crackers and a chunk of chocolate to create the Girl Scouts' classic s'more (see page 217).

As early as 2000 B.C., the ancient Egyptians were enjoying a gooey treat similar to what we now call marshmallows. Made from the sap of the mallow plant, which grows wild in marshes (hence the name), their version of the candy was sweetened with honey. It wasn't until the mid-1800s when candy makers, tired of the laborious process involved in making the sweets with sap, came up with a faster and easier recipe using cornstarch and gelatin instead. The modern marshmallow was born.

campfire songs

on top of spaghetti

On top of spaghetti, all covered with cheese,
I lost my poor meatball when somebody
  sneezed.
It rolled off the table, and onto the floor,
And then my poor meatball rolled out of the
  door.
It rolled down the garden, and under a bush,
And then my poor meatball was nothing but
  mush!
The mush was as tasty, as tasty could be,
And then the next summer it grew into a tree.
The tree was all covered, all covered with
  moss,
And on it grew meatballs, all covered with
  sauce.
So if you have spaghetti, all covered with
  cheese,
Hold onto your meatball, 'cause someone
  might sneeze.

clementine

In a cavern, in a canyon,
Excavating for a mine,
Lived a miner, forty-niner,
And his daughter, Clementine.
Chorus
Oh, my darling, oh, my darling,
Oh, my darling Clementine,
You are lost and gone forever,
Dreadful sorry, Clementine.
Light she was and like a fairy,
And her shoes were number nine,
Herring boxes without topses,
Sandals were for Clementine.
Chorus

Drove she ducklings to the water
Every morning just at nine,
Hit her foot against a splinter,
Fell into the foaming brine.
Chorus
Ruby lips above the water,
Blowing bubbles soft and fine,
But, alas, I was no swimmer,
So I lost my Clementine.
Chorus
Then the miner, forty-niner,
Soon began to peak and pine,
Thought he oughta join his daughter,
Now he's with his Clementine.
Chorus
There's a churchyard on the hillside
Where the flower grow and twine,
There grow roses 'mongst the posies,
Fertilized by Clementine.
Chorus
In my dreams she still doth haunt me,
Robed in garlands soaked in brine,
Though in life I used to hug her,
Now she's dead, I draw the line.
Chorus
Now you scouts may learn the moral
Of this tragic tale of mine,
Artificial respiration
Would have saved my Clementine.
Chorus
How I missed her, how I missed her,
How I missed my Clementine,
Till I kissed her little sister,
And forgot my Clementine.

oh, susanna!

I come from Alabama with my banjo on my
  knee,
I'm going to Louisiana, my true love for to see.
It rained all night the day I left, the weather it
  was dry
The sun so hot I froze to death, Susanna,
  don't you cry.
Chorus
Oh, Susanna, oh, don't you cry for me,
For I come from Alabama with my banjo on
  my knee.
I had a dream the other night, when
  everything was still;
I thought I saw Susanna dear, a coming down
  the hill.
A buckwheat cake was in her mouth, a tear
  was in her eye,
Says I, I'm coming from the south, Susanna,
  don't you cry.
Chorus

Americans buy more than 90 million pounds of marshmallows annually.

home on the range

Oh, give me a home where the buffalo roam,
Where the deer and the antelope play,
Where seldom is heard a discouraging word,
And the skies are not cloudy all day.
Chorus
Home, home on the range,
Where the deer and the antelope play,
Where seldom is heard a discouraging word,
And the skies are not cloudy all day.
Chorus
Where the air is so pure, and the zephyrs
   so free,
The breezes so balmy and light,
That I would not exchange my home on
   the range,
For all of the cities so bright.
Chorus
The Red man was pressed from this part of
   the west,
He's likely no more to return,
To the banks of the Red River where seldom
   if ever
Their flickering campfires burn.
Chorus
How often at night when the heavens are
   bright,
With the light from the glittering stars,
Have I stood there amazed and asked as
   I gazed,
If their glory exceeds that of ours.
Chorus
Oh, I love these wild flowers in this dear land
   of ours,
The curlew I love to hear cry,
And I love the white rocks and the antelope
   flocks,
That graze on the mountain slopes high.
Chorus

Oh, give me a land where the bright diamond
   sand,
Flows leisurely down in the stream;
Where the graceful white swan goes gliding
   along,
Like a maid in a heavenly dream.
Chorus
Then I would not exchange my home on
   the range,
Where the deer and the antelope play;
Where seldom is heard a discouraging word,
And the skies are not cloudy all day.

michael, row the boat ashore

Michael, row the boat ashore,
Hallelujah.
Michael, row the boat ashore,
Hallelujah.
Sister, help to trim the sails,
Hallelujah.
Sister, help to trim the sails,
Hallelujah.
River Jordan's deep and wide,
Hallelujah.
Milk and honey on the other side,
Hallelujah.
River Jordan's chilly and cold,
Hallelujah.
Chills the body, but warms the soul,
Hallelujah.

HOW TO catch trout

There are many books on the intricacies of fishing: saltwater, freshwater, types of fish, types of bait, lures, rods, locations—fishing is incredibly complicated for something that looks so easy! For the sake of simplicity—and because I love trout pan-fried—here's a quick-start guide to trout fishing.

» First, check with your town hall or a nearby tackle shop about purchasing a fishing license, and any rules and regulations you might need to follow. Get your hands on a freshwater fly-fishing pole and fishing gear, as well as the correct bait; trout love flies, salmon eggs, canned corn kernels, and worms.

» Trout live in fresh water—look for them in brooks, streams, lakes, and ponds. Approach the water quietly; try to keep your shadow from covering the water. Pick a remote rocky area, because trout often hide behind rocks in their search for food, and look for signs of fish in subtle changes in the water flow or the sight of a fin breaking the water's surface.

» To bait your hook with a worm, push the hook through the end of the worm and work the worm over the hook. Pull an inch or two of the worm past the hook's tip and allow it to dangle loosely. If you're using flies, corn, or salmon eggs, put a few pieces on the hook just past the barb.

» Place just enough weight on your line to allow the bait to bump the stream's bottom and float along, then cast upstream and let the line move downstream with the current. This is called the cast-and-retrieve method.

» When you feel a bite, set the hook by rapidly jerking the rod's tip up about 1 to 2 feet, then reel the fish in.

» If you plan to release your catch, handle it as little as possible (ideally, not at all) because touching a fish can damage the protective coating on its scales. To release, let the trout slip off the hook and go back into the water. Fish are easily injured, so be gentle; don't throw or drop it in the water.

HOW TO clean a fish

materials

- Cutting board or clean newspaper
- Sharp boning knife
- Spoon
- Fish scaler and blunt knife
- Filleting gloves (optional)

1. Wash the fish well with cold fresh water and place on a clean cutting board or newspaper.

2. With the sharp knife, cut the head off by slicing down behind the gills, then slice down the belly and remove the innards.

3. Remove the kidney line that runs along the spine by scraping it away with the rounded edge of a spoon.

4. Wash both the inside and outside of the fish in cold fresh water until clean.

SCALING

If you're not sure if you need to scale your fish, run the blade of a blunt knife at a 90-degree angle across the body, from the tail to the head. If the scales are thick and come up easily, you'll need to remove them. Grab the fish by the tail, and using short strokes from head to tail, scrape the fish with either a fish scaler or the edge of the knife until clean.

cornmeal-encrusted pan-fried trout

- Several brook trout or rainbow trout, cleaned, heads removed
- Salt and pepper to taste
- Coarse yellow cornmeal
- Butter or olive oil
- Lemon wedges

Sprinkle the trout inside and out with a bit of salt and pepper, then roll in cornmeal.

In a large skillet, melt the butter over medium-high heat, then add the fish and fry for about 3 to 5 minutes on each side (depending on the size), or until golden brown and the fish flakes easily with a fork.

Serve with lemon wedges. » makes 1 small trout per person.

THE HOODIE

My husband, who spent his childhood summers on Flying Point Beach in Southampton, Long Island, wore a much loved powder-blue hoodie, with SOUTHAMPTON spelled out in an arc of bold white letters across the chest, from 1972 when it was purchased, until its sad retirement to the ragbin in 1978. He has many fond memories of wearing it on cold, damp Long Island mornings, when he'd sneak out in the early hours with his father to grab the first batch of warm crullers from the world-famous Crutchley's Bakery in Southampton (see recipe) or on chilly evenings when his father would corral the whole family into the station wagon and bring them to the Sip'n Soda for juicy burgers and thick shakes.

One hundred and seventy-one miles to the southwest, on the New Jersey coastline, I was wearing a pink hoodie with an embroidered dolphin leaping across the chest. I wore it all summer long—to the Dairy Queen for dipped cones, to the beach to watch my father surf-fish, to play skeet ball at the arcades.

Southampton crullers

1 cup granulated sugar

2 large eggs, chilled

1 egg yolk, chilled

1½ teaspoons salt

½ cup chilled evaporated milk

½ cup ice water

3 teaspoons vanilla extract

4 cups all-purpose flour

4 teaspoons non-alum baking powder

2 teaspoons freshly ground nutmeg

¼ cup melted shortening

Shortening for deep frying

Superfine or confectioners' sugar

Using an electric mixer, beat the sugar, eggs, extra yolk and salt on high speed until creamy (about 2 minutes).

Add the milk, ice water, and vanilla, then lower the speed and gradually add the flour, baking powder, and nutmeg. Add the melted shortening (not too hot) and continue mixing at low speed until thoroughly blended.

Chill the batter in the refrigerator for 8 hours.

Remove the batter from the refrigerator and knead until pliable (approximately 4 to 5 minutes). With a rolling pin, roll the dough, using as little flour as possible, so it is less than ½ inch thick, then cut into rounds with a doughnut cutter or a small heart-shaped cutter.

Fry the pieces of dough in deep fat that registers 375° to 380°F., until they turn deep golden brown.

Drain on a rack until the crullers are room temperature, then dust with the superfine sugar or confectioners' sugar. Store in an airtight container.

》 makes approximately 4 dozen crullers

the perseid meteor shower

One night each year, in mid-August, we set the alarm clock for 3:00 A.M., shake the sleep out of our heads, then lumber outside with steaming mugs of coffee, to watch the amazing light show that is the Perseid meteor shower.

The Perseids, for those who have never watched them, are an annual shower associated with the comet Swift-Tuttle. Visible from mid-July to mid-August each year, the shower usually peaks between August 8 and August 14, during which point, hundreds of meteors per hour can be seen. It is truly spectacular!

Best observed from points in the Northern Hemisphere (and outside of large cities where lights and pollution don't dim the visibility), these "shooting stars" are made up of tiny dust particles that become extremely hot as they hit Earth's upper atmosphere at speeds of 20 to 50 miles per seconds, generating streaks of light across the night sky before they fade away.

tips for enjoying the light show

» While the Perseids extend from mid-July through mid-August and dates vary each year, most of the shower activity usually occurs between August 8 and 14, and the peak viewing nights are generally August 11, 12, and 13.

» The best viewing hours are between 2:00 A.M. and 4:00 A.M.

» On average, expect to see about one to three events per minute.

» It may be cool at night, so bring along warm sweatshirts or blankets as well as a thermos of coffee, tea, or cocoa to chase away the chill.

» A comfortable chair or pillow is essential if you're planning on gazing for more than a few minutes.

» Forget the camera and binoculars—they won't do much good. Instead, just sit or lie back and enjoy the show.

how to identify stars and constellations

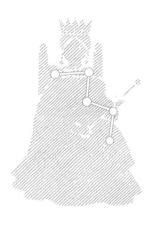

CASSIOPEIA

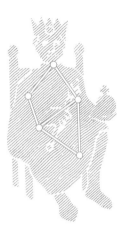

CEPHEUS

HERCULES

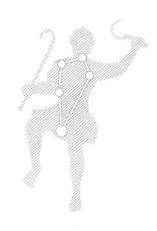

BOÖTES

SAGITTARIUS

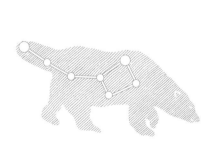

URSA MINOR/LITTLE DIPPER

URSA MAJOR/BIG DIPPER

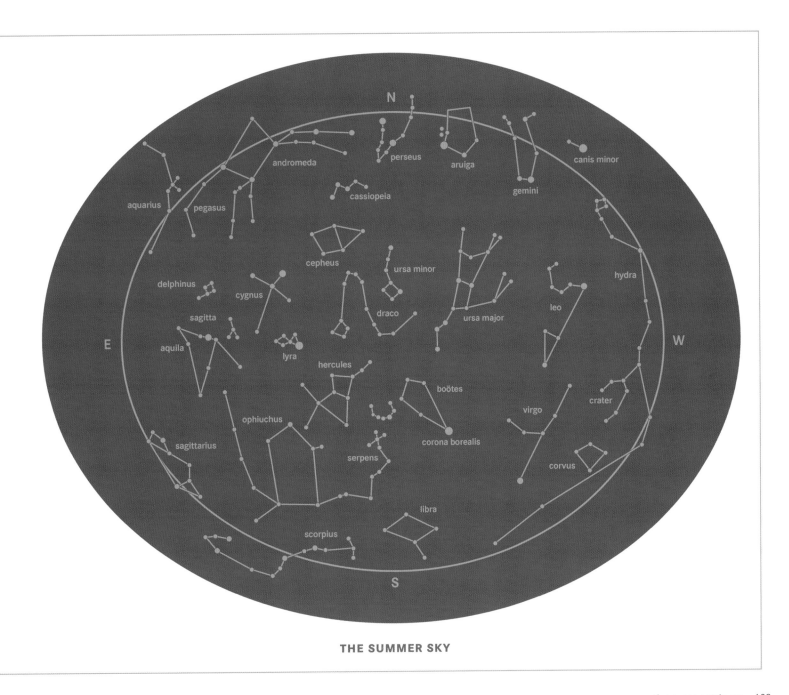

THE SUMMER SKY

games, indoors and out

Forget about the Olympics—the real games of summer are being played in backyards and living rooms across America. When the temperature climbs, low-key lawn games like badminton, croquet, bocce, and horseshoes are the perfect (relatively sweat-free) way to spend a late afternoon with friends. They're wonderful icebreakers as well; even if someone is new to the crowd, he or she can start socializing by getting in on the action. We've had our fair share of rousing and raucous bocce and horseshoe matches at our barbecues, some actually taking precedence over the meal itself and continuing late into the evening. That's not to say every backyard activity needs to be competitive; sometimes it's nice simply to toss a Frisbee around on the lawn in the early evening.

While backyard games keep our bodies active, indoor games challenge our minds. We all remember the board games of our childhood; we started out with Candyland, moving our gingerbread men through Molasses Swamp and Lollipop Woods, then we moved on to Monopoly, where (at least in my house) we'd argue over who would get to be the thimble or the top hat, who'd get stuck being the iron. Eventually, we matured enough to realize that Scrabble is not just for "old folks," and that chess is more interesting than it looks, and we had enough life experiences to actually get some of the answers to Trivial Pursuit correct.

We're big fans of board games in my household, and I'm always on the lookout for a new puzzle, game, or fun diversion for when the weather's less than perfect. A few years ago I introduced my sister-in-law Arlene to the game Jenga. The premise is simple: wooden blocks are stacked in a tower, and the players have to remove blocks from the bottom, and place them on top, without toppling the tower. It seems so easy—until you are in the middle of a nerve-wracking, white-knuckled, edge-of-your-seat match with my Jenga-obsessed sister-in-law! Our matches border on Olympian, but that's half the fun; the beauty of board games is that they not only help us to pass the time, but also bring us closer together with family and friends.

HOW TO play horseshoes

It's believed that horseshoes, or horseshoe pitching, was a budget-minded variation of the discus throw adapted by fans of the original Greek Olympic Games more than two thousand years ago. The rules were standardized and refined in England in the late 1800s, where the game evolved to closely resemble the version we play today. You can buy a horseshoe set—rubber or steel, including stakes—from most sporting goods stores.

setting up the court

1. Find a flat space about 6 feet wide by 46 feet long. If possible situate the court north-to-south, rather than east-to-west, to avoid having the sun in your eyes while playing.

2. Dig 3-foot square pits about 40 feet apart for the stakes. Fill the pits with sand or other soft fill to absorb the energy of the pitched horseshoes and insert the stakes; they should stand 14 to 15 inches above the surface of the pit

3. Draw foul lines 3 feet in front of the stakes for men, and 13 feet for women, children, and seniors.

how to play

» Each team has one or two players, and each player uses two horseshoes.

» The first player pitches both shoes. One of the opposing players then does the same. The second players on each team then take their turn. If playing in teams of two, teammates pitch from opposite sides toward each another. Players may not cross the foul line when pitching a horseshoe.

» Games are played to 40 points. Ties can be resolved by a tie-breaking round or two.

keeping score

A horseshoe must land within a one-horseshoe width of a stake to qualify to score. Follow these rules:

ACTION	POINTS
The horseshoe nearest the stake scores	1
Two horseshoes inside an opponent's shoes	2
A "ringer"—a toss that results in a horseshoe surrounding the stake, usually with satisfying "clang"	3
Ringers by opposing teams on a single stake	0
A "leaner"—a toss that leaves the horseshoe leaning on the stake	1

HOW TO PLAY croquet

Believed by many to have evolved from a French pastime known as Paille-Maille, a version of the game that would be called croquet was first played by thirteenth-century French peasants. The game eventually migrated to the Irish countryside, and was later adopted by the British leisure class, and renamed "croquet" or "crooked stick." Croquet rapidly caught on with British women and couples, and by the late 1800s it had spread to America, where it remains popular among casual and competitive players alike.

» Croquet is best played on a large grassy field upon which seven wickets (inverted hoops) are arranged into a double diamond pattern and two additional wickets and goal stakes are set at opposite ends of each of the diamonds. Croquet may also be played on a smaller single diamond course with a total of six wickets and two stakes.

» In standard play, players take turns hitting the balls around the course in a counterclockwise direction, and points are scored each time a ball is passed through a wicket or strikes a stake—but only when hit in the correct order and direction. Total points are calculated once both teams have completed the course, and the highest score wins. Alternatively, croquet can be played as a race, in which scores are completely disregarded and the first player to correctly complete the course wins.

» Croquet is played with four or six balls (two or three per side) and teams consisting of one to three players.

» Opposing teams play in rotation, with colored balls hit in the sequence indicated on the stakes, beginning with blue and ending with yellow.

» To begin, a player hits a ball toward the first wicket and is given a bonus stroke if the ball passes through. A player is also awarded a bonus stroke for hitting a stake.

» Whenever a struck ball comes to rest touching an opponent's ball (a condition know as a roquet), the striking player is given two bonus strokes. Only one roquet is awarded per turn, unless the ball first passes through a wicket. Also, consecutive croquets are not allowed against the same ball. A bonus stroke is often used to drive the opponent's ball into an unfavorable position.

» When both teams have completed the course, the score is tallied to determine the winner. For race-style play, the game ends when a player is the first to successfully complete the course.

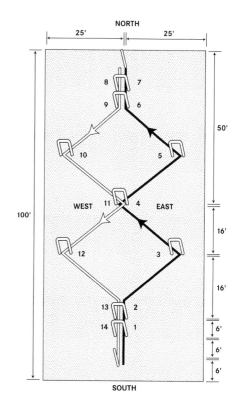

HOW TO MAKE A rope swing

Rope swings are usually found over swimming holes—picture swinging down into the water like Tarzan—but you can also install one on a sturdy branch in your backyard.

An extremely strong piece of rope 24 to 32 feet long

A lightweight rope as long as the swing rope (see below)

A ledge or bluff leading out to the water or a stout tree branch about 12 to 16 feet high

1. Using a figure 8 knot (see How to Tie a Sturdy Knot, page 80), create a loop about 5 to 8 inches in diameter at one end of the rope. Secure the Figure 8 with a stopper knot (see page 80). Double- and triple-check that this knot is secure.

2. Tie approximately eight double knots on the end of the rope opposite the loop at 2-foot intervals. These will provide an extra grip for your hands and feet while swinging.

3. Throw the loop end of the rope over the selected branch. You may need to attach a heavy object, such as a small log, or a plastic milk container filled with sand, to the rope to make for an easier throw; use extreme caution when doing so. Once you have both ends of the rope in your hands, slip the loose end of the rope through the loop in the opposite end. Pull the end without the loop through the loop and draw it up, securing the rope to the branch.

4. The addition of a retrieval line allows you to quickly remove the rope swing from the tree when it's not in use. Use a lightweight rope such as clothesline. Before pulling the rope swing through the loop (see above), secure a lightweight rope to the loop using a double half-hitch knot (page 80). When you're using the rope swing, tie the retrieval line off to the side to keep it out of the way. When you're finished, pull on the retrieval line to remove the swing from the tree.

SAFETY TIPS

» Make sure that the water around and beneath the swing is deep enough for a safe jump (at least 10 to 15 feet) and that there are no hidden rocks or other dangerous objects in the water.

» Never create or use a loop in the rope as a hold for your hands, feet, or any other part of your body while swinging, as you could easily get caught. Just hold on with your hands and feet.

» Make sure that children (and adults) know that they have to let go over the water and should never swing back on the rope.

HOW TO PLAY bocce

Scholars believe that a primitive form of the game that would eventually become bocce was first played by the Egyptians as far back as 5000 B.C., and was later adopted by the Greeks around 800 B.C. It's said that Galileo loved the sport for its blend of precision and competitive spirit and that Sir Francis Drake refused to launch a defense against the advancing Spanish Armada until he completed a game already in progress. Accounts of those said to have been on hand for what I imagine was one heck of a match claimed that Drake loudly exclaimed, "First we finish the game, and then we'll deal with the Armada!"

setting up the court

Find a flat, level place to set up the court. A court can be dirt, grass, gravel, or sand. The dimensions of the court should be approximately 10 to 13 feet wide and 60 to 100 feet long. In casual backyard play, adjust to fit your lawn.

the game

» To play, you will need two teams made up of one, two, or four players. The object of the game is to roll your bocce balls (*boccia*) closer to the smaller, white target ball (the *pallina*) than your opponents.

» Each team gets four like-colored bocce balls. If the teams have two or four players, everyone takes turns during each round.

» Once you decide which team throws first, the first player from the starting team tosses the pallina out toward the far end of the court. That player then rolls or tosses a boccia, trying to place it as close as possible to the pallina.

» Next, the opposing team takes a turn throwing the boccia, attempting to place it even closer to the pallina. Team members can use their boccia to knock an opposing team's ball away from the pallina, or to knock the pallina closer to their own boccia.

» The teams then alternate to throw their remaining balls and finish the round. A team is awarded one point for each boccia placed closer to the pallina than the opposing team; however, in the event of a tie, no points are awarded. The first team to reach 21 points wins, but it must win by 2, so the game can go past 21 if needed to determine a winner.

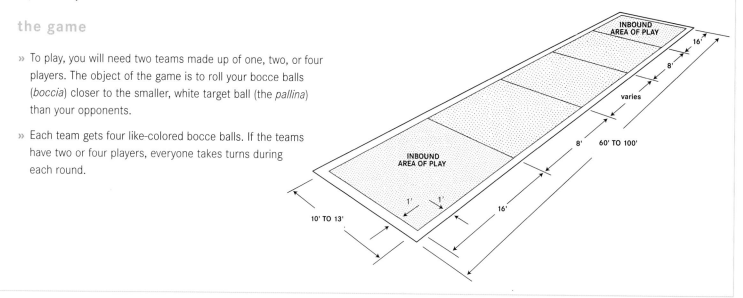

HOW TO PLAY badminton

Conjuring up images of charming Victorian lawn parties and tea sandwiches, badminton evolved out of a children's game called shuttlecock in 1873. And while a hard-struck shuttle can travel at speeds of up to 200 miles per hour, I prefer an easygoing approach to the game, with the shuttle lobbed in leisurely arcs high above the net.

» You will need two or four players, divided into two teams. Toss a coin to decide which team serves first.

» A server always serves from the right side and to the diagonal service box on the opposite side of the net. Serves are underhand only, and a server may not serve until his or her opponent is ready.

» Teams rally by hitting the shuttle or "birdie" back and forth over the net, each trying to l and it on the opposing team's court or to force an error. Points can be earned only by the serving team. If the nonserving team wins a rally, it gets no points but it does get to serve.

» Control of the serve is given to the nonserving team when it wins a point against the serving team.

» Points are scored when the shuttle is hit out of bounds or into the net or when a player touches the shuttle with any part of the body, or hits the shuttle before it crosses the net.

WHAT'S A SHUTTLECOCK?

A shuttlecock, or birdie, is the "ball" used in badminton. It has an open conical shape, with a rounded head that is traditionally made of cork and a skirt made of sixteen overlapping goose feathers. The best shuttlecocks are made from feathers from the left goose wing; apparently, for some unknown reason, shuttlecocks made from left feathers are usually more stable in flight. For casual backyard players, the cork-and-feathers have been replaced by a plastic or rubber head and plastic skirt.

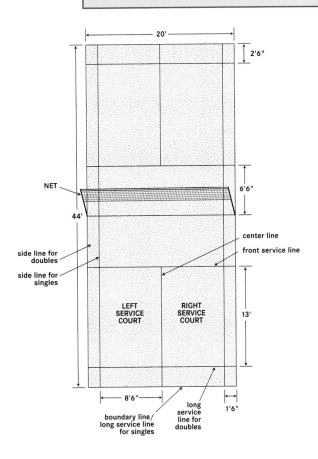

I was born into a baseball-obsessed family. My father's claim to fame was back in 1951, when during a local game, a bat somehow came in contact with his head, resulting in a weeklong coma and brain surgery. My mother remains convinced to this day that that knock to the head turned my father into a sort of baseball savant, since he can remember historical stats and scores as if he were there on the field himself. The next generation did him proud: my brother John became a minor celebrity in our hometown for pitching many no-hitters for his high school team (alas, a shoulder injury squelched his dreams of the big leagues), and my brother Michael was a gifted hitter. Even my mother and I were a part of the action, playing on local softball leagues in the summer months. So I guess it goes without saying that I come by my baseball passion rightfully. Our family loves to head to Yankee Stadium on warm evenings to cheer on the Boys of Summer.

American baseball as we know it was invented not by Abner Doubleday in 1839, but by Alexander Cartwright in 1845. Cartwright was twenty-five years old when he began playing a game known as town ball in a vacant lot in Manhattan. Forced from the lot by development, he and his friends moved across the Hudson River to Hoboken, New Jersey, and organized a ball club called the Knickerbockers. Seeking structure for this new sport, Cartwright came up with twenty basic rules that are to this day the backbone of modern-day baseball. Word spread, and soon another club—the New York Nine—was formed to challenge his team. On June 19, 1846, at Elysian Park in Hoboken, New Jersey, the Knickerbockers and the New York Nine played the first official baseball game on record. And while Cartwright was most likely embarrassed that his team fell to the Nine, 23–1, he would be proud to know that his passion started the revolution that is today known as the National Pastime.

rainy day movies

We have a library of movies that we turn to when there's nothing on TV or when the nasty weather keeps us indoors. Here are a few from our video library you might want to add to your own collection. Some are just for adults, others are perfect for kids.

want to laugh out loud?
Caddyshack
Animal House
There's Something About Mary
Austin Powers:
    International Man of Mystery
Big
Ferris Bueller's Day Off

need a shot of adrenaline?
True Lies
Spiderman
Raiders of the Lost Ark
King Kong (2005)
Independence Day
The Matrix

in the mood for love?
Pretty Woman
Sense and Sensibility
Sabrina (1954)
When Harry Met Sally
Down with Love
Love, Actually
The Princess Bride
Say Anything
Titanic
The Notebook

looking to be terrified?
The Exorcist
The Shining
Dawn of the Dead (2004)
The Blair Witch Project
The Birds
Friday the 13th

trying to keep the kids quiet?
Shrek
Ice Age
Finding Nemo
Toy Story
Mary Poppins
The Little Rascals (1994)
Willy Wonka and the Chocolate Factory

can't get enough of the classics?
Casablanca
The Graduate
Rear Window
Butch Cassidy and the Sundance Kid
To Kill a Mockingbird
The Sting
Breakfast at Tiffany's
Some Like It Hot

need a good tearjerker?
Beaches
Terms of Endearment
Ghost
Mask
Love Story
Steel Magnolias

want a classic summer movie?
Beach Blanket Bingo
Dirty Dancing
Grease
National Lampoon's Vacation
The Parent Trap (1961)
Summertime
Meatballs
One Crazy Summer

want to root for the home team?
Field of Dreams
The Bad News Bears (1976)
Breaking Away
A League of Their Own
The Endless Summer
Riding Giants

> Most popcorn comes in two basic shapes: snowflake and mushroom. Snowflake is used in movie theaters because it pops bigger. Mushroom is used for candy because it doesn't crumble.

italian popcorn

2 tablespoons olive oil

8 cups popped popcorn

1/3 cup finely grated Parmigiano-Reggiano cheese

Salt and pepper to taste

In a large bowl, evenly drizzle olive oil over hot popcorn, then toss with cheese, salt, and pepper. ▸ makes 8 cups

backyard movies

Bored with barbecue night? Why not try something fun and different, like a backyard movie night instead? It's the perfect way to watch a movie and enjoy a balmy summer evening with neighbors and friends.

» To get started, rent a projector, screen, and movie from a video or camera store and set it up in the backyard. Make sure there's plenty of room for guests to gather and move about freely (without knocking over the screen and/or projector).

» Have everyone contribute to the meal. Unfussy foods that are easy to eat are best when you're watching a movie. Try panini sandwiches, wraps, cups of chili with wedges of cornbread, or fried chicken. Where possible, try making foods to match the theme of the movie. (For example, if you're screening *Jaws,* make grilled mako kebabs for the adults and fish sticks for the kids; bake cupcakes for dessert, and top with blue icing and gummy sharks. Or, if you're screening *Pulp Fiction,* make "Big Kahuna" burgers and "Five Dollar" milk shakes.)

HERE ARE SOME MORE TIPS:

» Have guests bring blankets, lawn chairs, and pillows, and start the movie at sunset.

» Consider dressing the little ones in their pajamas in case they fall asleep early.

» Keep bug spray handy to ward off biting pests.

» Don't forget the popcorn!

> Each kernel of popcorn contains a tiny bit of water. When heated, the expansion of this water causes the corn to pop.

old-fashioned caramel popcorn

If you're a fan of Cracker Jack, you'll love this old-fashioned caramel corn recipe.

- 6 cups popped popcorn
- 1 cup plain, unsalted nuts (peanuts, almonds, or cashews all work well)
- 4 tablespoons butter
- 1 cup brown sugar
- ½ cup light corn syrup
- ⅛ cup molasses
- ¼ teaspoon salt

Preheat the oven to 250°F.

Combine the popcorn and nuts in a large metal bowl or on a cookie sheet, then place in the oven.

Combine all the remaining ingredients in a saucepan. Bring the mixture to a boil over medium heat, stirring constantly. When the mixture reaches the hard-ball stage (a candy thermometer should register 260°F.–this will take approximately 20 to 25 minutes), it should begin to turn dark brown.

Remove the popcorn and peanuts from the oven and working quickly (and carefully), drizzle the caramel on top. Place the mixture back in the oven for 15 minutes, mixing every 5 minutes, so that all the popcorn is coated.

Remove from the oven, allow to cool, then store in an airtight container for up to a week. » makes approximately 7 cups

note: If caramel hardens on your saucepan, pour boiling water over it to melt it off, then wash as usual.

HOW TO PLAY checkers

1. Red always moves first, so flip a coin or choose who will play red.

2. To set up the board, the red player places one red checker on each black square in the first three rows of squares. The black player places one black checker on each black square in the first three rows of squares. When complete, there will be twelve staggered checkers on each side of the board and two empty rows in the middle of the board.

3. The red player begins by moving one red checker forward diagonally onto an adjacent free black square.

4. Players then take turns moving one of their checkers diagonally, one square at a time. Single checkers may move in a forward direction only.

5. You can "jump" an opponent's checker if it sits in a square diagonally adjacent to your checker with an open square on the opposite side. To jump, move a checker over your opponent's checker and place it on the opposite open square. Take possession of your opponent's jumped checker and remove it from the checkerboard.

6. When a jump positions a checker to immediately jump one ("double jump") or more additional checkers, continue to jump as many checkers as apply during a single turn.

7. When a checker reaches the opposite side of the board, it becomes a "king." A checker is "kinged" when the opponent stacks one of your previously jumped checkers on top of the kinged checker. Unlike single checkers, kings may move both forward and backward.

8. The first player to eliminate all of their opponent's checkers from the board wins the game. A player also wins if the opponent is blocked in such a way that prevents any legal move.

HOW TO PLAY solitaire

Solitaire, known as Patience in England, has an uncertain history, but is believed by many to have its origins in France; in fact, many early versions of the game were named after Napoleon, who was an avid player. Today there are many forms of Solitaire, including the ubiquitous computer-based version. Here's a set of basic rules.

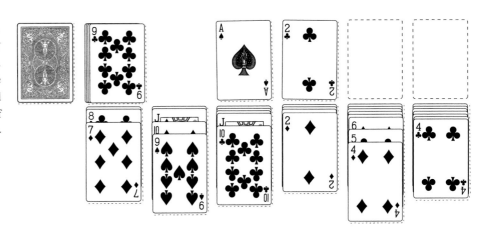

object of the game

To place every card in the deck into ordered piles of each of the four suits: hearts, diamonds, clubs, and spades.

setting up

Shuffle the deck thoroughly, and lay seven cards down in a horizontal row with the first card on the left face up, and the remaining cards face down.

Next, beginning with the second card (immediately to the right of the face-up card), lay another card on each of the six already on the table. Once again, the first card dealt should be face up and the rest face down.

Continue in this manner, in each case placing a face-up card followed by face-down cards. Proceed until twenty-eight cards have been dealt into seven stacks, each topped by a face-up card. Twenty-four cards now remain in the deck.

playing the game

Deal three cards from the remaining twenty-four cards into a pile, with the first two positioned face down, and the third face up. Examine the face-up card to see if it can be played. Cards are played onto the original row by creating overlapping layers of alternating colored cards (black/red/black) in descending sequence. For example, a four of clubs can be placed on a five of hearts. As aces are exposed, place them face up in a new row above the primary playing row. Same-suit cards are placed in ascending sequence on the final piles as they turn up throughout the game.

If the exposed card cannot be played, turn it back over and deal three more cards, again exposing the face of the third. If it can be played, do so, and continue by flipping the card beneath it face up.

As play continues, entire piles of exposed cards may be moved from one stack to another in the playing rows. For example, an exposed pile of cards beginning with a red seven can be moved on top of a pile with an exposed black eight.

The game continues until the player has gone through the deck three times, until no further moves can be made, or until all the cards end up in the final piles—in which case the player wins.

HOW TO PLAY 5-card draw poker

First introduced in the United States in the early 1800s by French settlers in New Orleans, poker later became extremely popular with the pioneers and gunslingers in the saloons and parlors of the Old West—yes, just like in the movies.

fundamentals of play

CARD RANKING

Poker uses a regular fifty-two-card deck. Card ranks, from the highest to the lowest, are ace (an ace can also be used as the lowest card), king, queen, jack, 10, 9, 8, 7, 6, 5, 4, 3, and 2. The suits are hearts, diamonds, clubs, and spades.

HANDS

In Poker, a "hand" is a series of five cards dealt to a player. The player with the highest-ranked hand wins the round. In order of lowest to highest rank, Hands in 5-Card Draw Poker are: a pair, two pair, three of a kind, a straight, a flush, a full house, four of a kind, a straight flush, and a royal flush.

BASICS OF FIVE-CARD DRAW POKER

The "ante" is made by everyone playing at the opening of a round. To "open" is to place the first bet in a round. "Seeing" is matching a bet to stay in the game, and "raising" is adding money to increase a bet. "Checking" is staying in the game but not betting (can be done only if a bet has not yet been placed), and "calling" is matching a bet to end a hand to determine the winner. "Folding" is quitting a round.

playing the game

1. To begin a round, each player antes up into the "pot."

2. The dealer shuffles the deck and working counterclockwise, deals each player a card face down until every player has five cards. The dealer then places the deck face down on the table.

3. The player to the left of the dealer may place an opening bet or pass.

4. Moving counterclockwise from the first player, each player in sequence may see, raise, or fold if a bet has been placed, or check (to check is to bet zero) if a bet has not yet been placed and that player does not want to open.

5. When each player has bet or folded, the remaining players may discard up to three cards and are dealt an equal number of new cards in an effort to improve a hand.

6. A new round of betting then begins, and players may open or check. Once a bet has been placed, each subsequent player may see, raise the bet, or fold.

7. A round ends when every player has either folded or no one raises the bet. At the end of the round, each player who has not folded shows his or her hand to determine the winner.

8. The player with the highest-ranked hand wins all the money in the pot.

9. Play continues until the players decide to stop.

RANKINGS	
A pair	Two cards of the same rank from different suits
Two pair	Two unique pairs in a hand
Three of a kind	Three cards of the same rank from different suits
A straight	Five cards of different suits in an unbroken sequence
A flush	Five nonsequential cards belonging to the same suit
A full house	Combination of a three of a kind and a pair
Four of a kind	Four cards of the same rank from different suits
A straight flush	A same-suit straight
A royal flush	An ace-high straight flush (the highest possible hand)

When playing poker, there's a 1-in-500 chance of drawing a flush.

HOW TO PLAY dominoes

When Bob Marley sang about "one love" there's a good chance he was singing of Jamaica's love of dominoes. Although believed to have originated in China, dominoes have become something of a national obsession on that Caribbean island. So, take a "trip" to Kingston this summer—grill up some jerk chicken, grab a few Red Stripes, and whittle away the afternoon playing a few rounds of Jamaica's favorite pastime.

» Dominoes are played by two, three, or four players.

» There should be twenty-eight dominoes in your set, ranging from double blank to double six. Place them all face down on the table and shuffle them until they're well mixed.

» Each player selects a single domino; the player with the highest total face value will play first. The dominoes are replaced and reshuffled.

» In a game of two, each player selects seven dominoes each. For three or four players, each player begins with five dominoes. Players keep the domino faces hidden from their opponents.

» The first player begins by turning a domino face up. Moving clockwise, the next player turns over a domino with a like value of one of the open ends of the first domino, and lays it alongside the first, making sure like-valued ends touch.

» Whenever a player cannot match an open end, he or she draws new dominoes from the pile until a match is found. If there are no more dominoes left in the pile, the player passes.

» The winner of each round is the first player to run out of dominoes. If everyone in a round passes, the winner is the person with the lowest score—scores are determined by adding up the number of dots on your remaining tiles. The winner of each round is awarded a number of points equal to the sum of the dots on the dominoes held by all the opposing players.

» Games are played to fifty points for two players or one hundred points for games of three or more players.

HOW TO PLAY charades

Charades originated in France in the eighteenth century, and eventually became a popular parlor game in Victorian England. The game works best when played by at least six players divided into two teams.

» Divide the participants into two equal teams. Agree upon a time limit for each round and the number of rounds to be played. Three or four minutes per player per round is recommended.

» Separate the teams so they can't hear each other. Have each think up a series of short phrases such as titles of movies, books, and TV shows, popular catchphrases, and common sayings. The phrases shouldn't be obscure or in a foreign language; use appropriately simple phrases if children are playing.

» Each phrase should be written on a separate scrap of paper. The papers are collected and placed in a glass bowl (one for each team). Each team then gets the opposite team's bowl.

» The first player selects a piece of paper from the bowl, reads it silently, and keeps the phrase in mind. Without speaking, that player then acts out the phrase while teammates attempt to guess the phrase.

» A turn ends either when the phrase is guessed correctly or time runs out. The teams take turns for the desired number of rounds. A tally of correct answers and the time required to answer should be kept. The team with the most correct answers, or the one that answers in the least amount of time for all the rounds, wins.

SIGNALING TIPS AND TRICKS

Number of words	To indicate the number of words in the title, hold up the appropriate number of fingers.
Book	To signal a book, put your hands together as if praying, and then unfold them as if a book.
Television	To signal a television show, draw a box in the air with your finger.
Quote	To signal a quote, make quotation marks in the air with your fingers.
"Sounds like"	To indicate that something "sounds like" something else, tug your earlobe.
Short word/long word	Pinch your thumb and forefinger together for a short word, or open them up to indicate a longer word.
Correct answer	Let your teammates know they have guessed a word correctly by tapping your index finger on the tip of your nose and pointing to the person who guessed correctly.
Getting warmer/colder	To let your teammates know they're getting closer to the correct answer, wipe your hand across your forehead. If they're getting further, cross your arms and pretend to shiver.

fictionary

This is a game we love to play with guests. It's fun for adults and kids and always stirs up lots of head-slapping and giggling—a sure sign of success.

    A large, unabridged dictionary
    Pencils or pens
    Index cards for each player

In this game, players guess the definition of an obscure word. A turn consists of one player choosing a word from the dictionary and all other players creating fake, but believable, definitions. The round is over when each player has taken a turn picking a word to be guessed. Players receive 1 point for voting for the correct definition and 1 point for each vote their fake definition receives. If no one selects the correct definition, the player who chose the word earns 3 points.

1. One player chooses a word from the dictionary, reads it to the group, and spells it aloud (if someone is familiar with the word a new word must be selected).

2. While the word-picker copies down the dictionary definition, each player writes a credible-sounding definition for the word.

3. The word-picker collects all definitions and reads them aloud once, in any order. On a second reading, players must vote for the definition that they think is correct (the word-picker should keep track of the votes).

4. After points are tallied, the dictionary gets passed to another player, who then chooses the next word.

We usually start by deciding how many rounds to play, and whoever has the most points at the end wins. You'd be surprised how good kids are at this game! Having guests is a great reason to play; it's most fun with a big group. If you've never played before, tune into the quiz show *Says You!* on your local National Public Radio station, where Fictionary is featured as a weekly segment.

Here are some real two-letter words from the fifth edition of *The Official Scrabble Players Dictionary*. Two-letter words are the key to increasing your score—and there are a lot more of them than *at, it,* and *on.* Use them to make two words on one turn or block another player from getting a triple word score. Knowing the definitions won't score you any points on the board, but it may with your friends!

» aa	» ef	» mm	» re
» ab	» el	» mo	» sh
» ae	» em	» mu	» si
» ag	» en	» na	» ta
» ai	» er	» ne	» ti
» al	» es	» nu	» un
» am	» et	» od	» ut
» ar	» ex	» oe	» wo
» aw	» fe	» oi	» xi
» ay	» hm	» op	» xu
» ba	» ka	» os	» ya
» bi	» ki	» ow	» ye
» bo	» li	» oy	» yo
» de	» lo	» pe	» za
» ed	» mi	» qi	

the summer table

Usually just around the time the first crocuses start popping their

their colorful heads out of the soil, I've pretty much had my fill of winter's rutabagas, turnips, and brussels sprouts, and I start longing for a sweet, buttery ear of corn, or a bowl of luscious black cherries. Cold weather foods may be meant to warm our souls, but summer foods are meant to restore them.

In my opinion, the best summer meals are a little messy (think sticky ribs, juicy burgers), totally stress-free (break out the grill and paper napkins), and require minimal ingredients (the focus being on freshness, not fussiness). In fact, I will go so far as to say that the best-kept secret about summer entertaining is that it's pretty hard to screw it up—so don't be intimidated about inviting friends over for casual meals.

The following are my seasonal favorite recipes that I turn to time and again because they are not only easy to make, but crowd-pleasers as well; I have yet to meet a person who doesn't love dipping warm corn chips into a bowl of fresh guacamole, or who doesn't let out a sincere "mmm . . ." when taking a bite out of a sweet lobster roll. But don't be afraid to experiment with new ingredients and recipes, especially since the local farmer's market can offer plenty of surprises: try using duck eggs for your next fresh herb omelet, gooseberries in your next summer pudding, wild boar sausage on your next "everything but the kitchen sink" pizza. You'll be amazed at how good freshness tastes.

drinks and cocktails

arlene's sangria

- 1.5 liter bottle red wine (cabernet sauvignon, merlot, rioja, zinfandel, shiraz)
- 2 tablespoons sugar—superfine is best
- Splash of orange juice
- 1 lemon, cut into slices
- 1 orange, cut into slices
- 1 apple, cut into thin wedges
- 2 shots brandy
- Soda water

In a large pitcher, mix together the wine, sugar, juice, and fruit, and refrigerate for 24 hours. When ready to serve, stir in the brandy and thin slightly with soda water. Serve sangria over ice. » serves 6 to 8

sea breeze cocktail

- 1 ounce grapefruit juice
- 4 ounces cranberry juice
- 1 ounce vodka

Combine both the juices and the vodka in a shaker with ice. Shake well, and strain into an ice-filled highball glass.

Sip under a palm tree. » serves 1

mint julep

Best known for its appearance at the annual Kentucky Derby, where more than 80,000 mint juleps are served over the course of the two-day event, the drink is traditionally served in a silver julep cup. Since most households I know of (including mine) don't have one in the cabinet, a Collins glass is an acceptable substitute.

- 1 cup water
- 1 cup sugar
- 6 to 7 mint leaves, plus additional for garnish
- 3 ounces bourbon
- Crushed ice

Make a simple syrup by bringing the water and sugar to a boil. Allow it to cool. (Leftover syrup can be stored indefinitely in the refrigerator.)

When ready to serve, place the mint leaves in a julep or Collins glass. Add ½ ounce of the syrup and muddle. Add the bourbon and crushed ice.

Garnish your cocktail with mint leaves. Serve with straws. » serves 1

mojito

Pronounced moh-HEE-toh, this popular Cuban cocktail is perfect for using up that endless supply of mint your garden produces.

- ½ lime
- 10 fresh mint leaves
- 3 teaspoons sugar
- Crushed ice
- 1½ ounces rum
- 2 ounces club soda
- 1 sprig of mint for garnish (optional)

Squeeze the juice of ½ lime into a tall glass. Add the mint leaves and sugar, then muddle (or stir to crush) the leaves to extract their flavor.

Add the crushed ice, rum, and club soda and stir well to blend. Garnish with a sprig of mint if desired. » serves 1

hurricane cocktail

This cocktail was concocted during World War II at the legendary Pat O'Brien's bar in the French Quarter of New Orleans. In those days, whiskey was in short supply, so a clever bartender came up with this fruity—yet potent—drink using different types of rum instead. The drink is named after the glass it's served in, which resembles a hurricane lamp.

2 ounces dark rum

2 ounces light rum

2 ounces passion fruit juice

1/2 ounce fresh lime juice

1 ounce orange juice

1 tablespoon grenadine

Ice

1 slice of orange (optional)

2 marsachino cherries (optional)

Add the rums, juices, and grenadine into a cocktail shaker with ice, then shake well. Strain into a large, ice-filled glass, then garnish with an orange slice and cherries, if desired. » serves 1

piña colada

Creamy, smooth, and delicious. Hawaii in a glass.

3 ounces light rum

3 ounces pineapple juice

2 ounces cream of coconut

3/4 cup ice

1 slice of pineapple for garnish (optional)

1 maraschino cherry for garnish (optional)

Place the rum, juice, and cream of coconut in a blender with the ice. Blend on high speed until creamy and smooth.

Pour into a tall glass, garnish with a slice of pineapple and a cherry, and serve with a straw. » serves 1

margarita

1 1/2 ounces tequila

1 ounce Cointreau

1 ounce fresh lemon juice

1 ounce fresh lime juice

Kosher salt (optional)

Sliced limes for garnish (optional)

Add all the ingredients and ice to a cocktail shaker, shake well, then strain into a margarita glass. Garnish with a slice of lime if you are using it. » serves 1

VARIATIONS

» If you prefer your margarita with salt, begin by pouring salt into a small dish. Moisten rim of chilled cocktail glass with sliced lime, and dip into salt.

» For a frozen version, place all ingredients in a blender with ice and mix until smooth. Pour into a margarita glass, garnish with a slice of lime, and enjoy.

» If you prefer a fruity, frozen margarita, simply add a handful of strawberries, some sliced mango, a splash of peach nectar, or whatever kind of summery fruit or fruit juice you have handy, and blend with ice.

Do you know what a good margarita does to seemingly ordinary people on hot August afternoons? It makes them want another.

That odd marriage of bitter tequila, sweet orange liqueur, puckery lime, and crunchy salt is nearly addictive. Whether it's shaken, stirred, blended with ice, mixed with fruit, served straight up, with salt or without, there's no topping the margarita as the official cocktail of summer. Consider it sunshine in a glass.

Although there are many theories about its origins, the most popular one is that Dallas socialite Margarita Sames created it in 1948 at her vacation home in Acapulco, Mexico. It was a splashing success with her guests and rapidly caught on with the social elite of Texas and Hollywood. The rest, as they say, is history.

summer treats

beach bar mahimahi sandwich

We pedal our bikes for miles down the beach, stopping halfway for a simple beach bar lunch to keep us going. Our favorite is this grilled fish sandwich, served on a soft roll and topped with a thick slice of tomato and a spoonful of tartar sauce.

6 mahimahi skinless fillets, each 6 ounces each, 1 inch thick

3 tablespoons olive oil

Salt and pepper to taste

2 lemons, quartered

6 hamburger buns or hard rolls

Tartar sauce (page 142)

Sliced tomato (optional)

Coat the fish with the olive oil. Season with salt and pepper. Over a medium-hot grill, grill the fish 4 to 5 minutes, on each side.

When the fish is done, give it a squeeze or two of lemon, place on hamburger buns, and top off with a spoonful of tartar sauce and, if desired, sliced tomato. » makes 6 sandwiches

spicy cashews

1 tablespoon vegetable oil

2 cups cashews

2 teaspoons paprika

1 teaspoon chili powder

¼ teaspoon cayenne pepper

Pour the vegetable oil into a preheated wok or skillet. Add the remaining ingredients and stir constantly for 1 to 2 minutes.

Drain the spiced cashews on paper towels and cool before serving. » serves 4; makes 2 cups

3 ESSENTIAL CDS FOR BEACH BAR LISTENING

Meet Me in Margaritaville, Jimmy Buffett

Caribbean Steeldrums: 20 Famous Tropical Melodies—Calypso, Samba, Various Artists

The Best of Studio One, Vol. 1, Various Artists

cantina guacamole

Adding minced jalapeños to this recipe will spice it up; chopped cilantro will give it a real South of the Border flavor.

- 2 plum tomatoes
- 2 firm-ripe California avocados
- 2 tablespoons minced red onion
- 3 tablespoons fresh lime juice
- Salt and pepper to taste

Quarter the tomatoes, remove the seeds, and chop. Set aside.

Halve and pit the avocados, scoop the flesh into a bowl, and mash (you can use your hands, a masher, or a mortar and pestle). Stir in the tomatoes, red onion, and lime juice.

Season with salt and pepper. » makes 2 cups

note » Avocados turn brown when exposed to the air. To help keep your guacamole from turning brown (or at least stall the inevitable), insert the avocado pit into the center of the prepared guacamole, squeeze some lemon or lime over the top, and keep it well covered with plastic wrap before serving.

classic summerhouse lemonade

Few things quench a summer thirst like a puckery glass of lemonade. I like mine with crushed ice. Add a splash of grenadine for the pink version.

- 7 cups water
- 2 cups fresh-squeezed lemon juice (about 8 to 12 large lemons)
- 1 cup or more sugar to taste
- Ice cubes or crushed ice
- Lemon slices (optional)

In a large pitcher, mix the water and lemon juice. Add the sugar slowly, mixing well to make sure it all dissolves, then refrigerate.

When ready to serve, pour into an ice-filled glass and garnish with fresh lemon slices, if you are using them. » serves 6

citrus sun tea

Every summer I set out a jar of this orange-flavored tea to brew in the warmth of the sun. If you don't have orange juice on hand, it's fine to omit.

materials

- Large glass jar with lid

ingredients

- 14 tea bags
- 8 cups cold water
- 1 cup fresh orange juice
- Handful of fresh mint leaves, plus additional for garnish (optional)
- 1 lemon, quartered
- 1–2 cups sugar
- Orange slices for garnish (optional)

In a large glass jar, combine the tea bags, water, juice, mint, and lemon. Add sugar to taste, screw on the cap, and shake gently to mix the ingredients. Place the jar in a warm, sunny location for approximately 3 hours.

Remove the tea bags and lemon and serve the sun tea over ice. If you'd like, garnish each glass with an orange slice and a sprig of mint. » serves 6

THE NEW ENGLAND CLAMBAKE

Pity the poor soul who hasn't experienced a classic New England clambake in the golden glow of a summer sunset. We have the Native Americans of coastal New England to thank for this simple meal in which alternating layers of clams, potatoes, lobsters, and corn are separated by seaweed, then steam-baked in a rock-lined firepit.

Traditionally held on the beach, clambakes are all-day social events, as it takes hours for the meal to cook—but that's half the fun. My family has thrown an annual clambake for as long as I can remember, and the day's events are usually just as memorable as the bake itself: we comb the beach for treasures, play horseshoes or bocce, and splash in the ocean, stopping only to slurp down a few raw oysters or take a sip of a cold microbrew. Then finally, at the end of the day—with the setting sun as our backdrop—we all gather around the campfire and enjoy the fruits of our labor. (For instructions on having a clambake, see pages 144 and 145.)

DIGGING FOR DINNER
a guide to clamming

We grew up eating the clams we foraged for, so it seems perfectly natural to me to head to the beach at low tide to dig some up for dinner. For those of you who are lucky enough to live or vacation in an area that has edible clams, and want to try your hand—or feet—at clamming, there are a few things you'll need to do in preparation.

» First, contact the local town hall to find out if the clams in your area are okay to eat, if you need a license or permit, and if there are any rules and regulations you need to follow. Second, decide what kind of clamming you want to do—treading or raking.

» Treading means you use your feet to feel for clams buried in the sand; simply get into the water and twist your feet into the mud. It's a smart idea to wear a pair of water shoes to prevent your feet from getting cut. To rake for clams, you'll need a scratch rake, which you can buy at fish and tackle shops. To dig, stand in the water and rake back and forth in the mud until you feel a clam, then scoop it up.

» Whichever method you choose, you'll need a bucket to hold your clams; one with holes in the bottom lets the water drain and helps keep the bucket afloat.

» Once you're back home, make sure your live clams stay cold and get plenty of oxygen. The best way to store them is to put them in a colander, then set the colander inside a large bowl, which will catch drips and allow air circulation. Next, lay some slightly dampened paper towels over them and store them in the coldest area of your refrigerator—*not* the freezer. Consume them within one or two days.

TIPS FOR A SUCCESSFUL DIG

» The best time to dig is just after low tide.
» You don't have to dig to China to find clams; they live fairly close to the surface.
» If the water is very cold, consider investing in a pair of waders.
» If there are no other people around, don't clam alone. Deep muck can be dangerous, and the last thing you want is to get stuck in it.
» If others are digging around you, practice good clamming etiquette. Don't throw clams that are too small into their path; toss them into the ocean instead. The same goes for dirt and seaweed—watch where you're flinging it.
» After digging, fill in your holes.
» Before heading home, rinse your catch to remove any mud or sand.

Clams are divided into two groups: soft-shell and hard-shell. The former grow in muddy coastal areas; the latter live in sandy bays and along beaches. While there are hundreds of types of both, here are some of the most popular.

butter » From the Puget Sound area, these are small, sweet clams that can be eaten raw or cooked. (They're also called money shells—Native Americans used them as money.)

geoduck » This Pacific clam is the largest burrowing clam in the world, weighing between two and four pounds. It can be shucked and sautéed, and it makes a tasty chowder.

manila » Imported from Asia in the 1930s, this variety of littleneck is now a dominant species in the Northwest. They can be served raw, but are most often steamed.

pismo » Named for the coastline city of Pismo Beach, California, where they were first found, these are sweet and tender, and very scarce. The connector muscle can be served raw; the body meat is usually steamed or deep-fried.

quahog » An East Coast favorite, quahogs can range from about 1½ to 6 inches across. The largest are sometimes called chowder clams; they can be tough and are best cut up and added to soups. The smaller ones are called cherrystones or littlenecks. Cherrystones measure less than 3 inches across, littlenecks about 2 to 2½ inches. They're great served raw, but can be cooked as well.

razor » These popular West Coast clams are named for their resemblance to an old-fashioned straight razor and the sharpness of their shells. They are most often steamed.

steamer » This soft-shelled Eastern clam, also known as the Ipswich clam, is recognizable by the long siphon that projects from its thin shell. As the name suggests, it's usually steamed, but it can also be shucked, battered, and deep-fried.

HOW TO shuck clams and oysters

Once you get the basic steps down, shucking becomes second nature. You'll need a good pair of shucking gloves (a towel will do in a pinch), a stiff brush, and a clam or oyster knife.

» Work only with live shellfish. They should be tightly closed. If they're open slightly, tap them; if they don't react to your touch, discard them. Also discard any with cracked shells.

» With a stiff brush, scrub the clams or oysters under cold running water. Then hold one clam or oyster in the palm of your hand, with a shucking glove or towel protecting your palm. You may want to work over a large bowl to catch the juices.

FOR CLAMS

Brace the clam's "hinge" against the meaty part of your palm near your thumb. Carefully work the knife into the part of the shell near your fingertips, then slide it around the shell so that you cut the muscle at its hinge. Open the shell, scrape the meat from the top into the bottom, and serve.

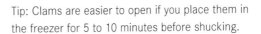

Tip: Clams are easier to open if you place them in the freezer for 5 to 10 minutes before shucking.

FOR OYSTERS

Position the oyster in your hand with the curved side facing down and the flatter side facing up. Work the knife into the part of the shell near the back hinge, then slide it around the shell so that you cut the muscle at its hinge. Twist the blade to separate the top and bottom shells, being careful not to spill the juices. Scrape the meat from the top shell into the bottom and serve.

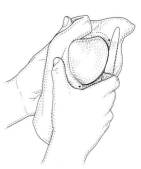

new haven-style clam pizza on the outdoor grill

While you certainly don't need them to get great results, a baker's peel (that wooden, paddlelike tool you see at a pizzeria) and a pizza stone are relatively inexpensive investments that make for a better pizza-making experience: the peel helps you transfer the pie, and the stone provides a hot, flat surface that cooks the crust evenly. (In a pinch, you can use a sheet of aluminum foil for both the transferring and the cooking, but the results won't be quite as good.) As for the dough, while homemade does taste better, far be it from me to tell you to stay in making dough on a beautiful summer day; if you're short on time (or would rather be outside having fun), head to the refrigerated section of your supermarket or to your local pizzeria and purchase it.

Thanks to my good friend, Matt Storch, chef at the wonderful Match Restaurant in Norwalk, Connecticut, for his help with grilling pizza.

1 teaspoon sugar

1 cup warm water (approximately 95°F)

¼ ounce package active dry yeast

2 to 2¾ cups all-purpose flour

2 teaspoons salt

¼ cup olive oil

Coarse cornmeal

1 to 1½ tablespoons chopped garlic

20 to 30 littleneck clams, shucked and chopped, or two 6½-ounce cans of chopped clams (reserve some juice)

2 to 3 tablespoons freshly grated Parmigiano-Reggiano cheese

½ teaspoon dried oregano, crumbled

Cracked black pepper to taste

In a small bowl dissolve the sugar in ¼ cup warm water, then sprinkle the yeast over the water and let sit for approximately 5 minutes, or until foamy. In a large bowl, mix together 2 cups flour, the remaining ¾ cup water, the salt, and the yeast mixture. Transfer the dough to a floured surface and knead with your hands, adding just enough of the remaining ¾ cup flour so that the dough becomes soft and smooth (not too sticky, not too dry).

Transfer the dough to a large, lightly oiled bowl, brush the top of the dough with a bit of olive oil to keep it moist, then cover the bowl with plastic wrap and set it in a warm place for 2 to 3 hours, or until it doubles in size.

When dough has doubled, gently press down in the center of the dough with your fist, remove it from the bowl and either wrap in plastic wrap to store in the refrigerator for future use (it will keep for about 24 to 36 hours) or place on a floured surface to use immediately.

Preheat the gas grill to 600°F., place the pizza stone on the rack, and close the top for at least 15 minutes to heat the stone. (If you are cooking this on a charcoal grill, or a grill without a built-in thermometer, use a barbecue thermometer to achieve the correct temperature. If you are cooking it in the oven, set the temperature to 500°F.).

Flatten the dough out on a lightly floured surface, and using your hands or a rolling pin, carefully stretch the dough out to form a very thin, flat circle (thin is key for a light, crispy crust). Sprinkle the baker's peel with cornmeal, carefully slide the dough onto it, and cover with a clean dish towel for 10 to 15 minutes.

When ready to cook, brush the dough with olive oil, and top with the chopped garlic, the chopped clams and a bit of the reserved liquid, the grated cheese, the oregano, and the cracked black pepper. Carefully slide the pizza off the peel onto the hot pizza stone, and close the lid to the grill (or the door to the oven). Try not to open the lid too much, as you don't want the heat to escape. Bake the pizza 8 to 15 minutes (this will vary depending on the heat of your grill or oven, and the thickness of your dough), or until the bottom of the crust is medium-brown. When done, carefully remove the cooked pizza from the stone with spatulas, allow to cool for 1 minute, then slice into wedges. » serves 2 as an entrée, 4 to 6 as an appetizer

note » You can also split the dough to make two smaller pies.

fried clams (or oysters)

1 egg, beaten

1½ cups evaporated milk

¼ cup water

1 cup flour

1 cup fine cornmeal

Vegetable or peanut oil

6 cups shucked clams
  (best are soft-shell clams like
  steamer or Ipswich clams)

Tartar Sauce (page 142)

2 lemons, quartered

In a mixing bowl, beat together the egg and the evaporated milk. Top off with the water.

In another mixing bowl, combine the flour and cornmeal.

In a large pot or wok, heat enough oil to completely cover the clams until it reaches 350°F.

Dip the clams in the milk mixture, give them a quick shake to remove any excess liquid, then dip them in the flour mixture.

Carefully place the clams in the hot oil. Fry 1 to 2 minutes, or until deep golden brown. Then, using a slotted spoon, remove the clams from the oil and drain on paper towels or brown paper bags. Keep the cooked clams warm in a preheated oven set at 200°F. while you cook the rest.

When done, serve the clams with tartar sauce and lemon wedges. » serves 6

garlic-steamed clams

4 dozen hard-shelled clams,
  well scrubbed

3 tablespoons olive oil

10 cloves garlic, peeled and minced

½ cup water

½ cup wine

½ cup parsley, chopped

Lemon

Make certain your clams and oysters are alive by checking to see that they are tightly closed. If they are open slightly, tap to see if they react to your touch; if not, discard. Also discard any clams that have cracked shells. When ready to cook, scrub the clams with a stiff brush under cold running water.

In a large stockpot or Dutch oven with a lid, heat the olive oil, then add the garlic, and sauté for approximately 5 minutes.

Turn up the heat and add the water, the wine, and the parsley. Add the clams, close the lid, and allow the clams to steam for about 10 to 15 minutes, or until the clams open. (During the cooking process—without opening the lid—shake the pot a few times to redistribute the clams.)

When the clams are done, place them and their broth in a large bowl, discarding any clams that did not open. Squirt some lemon juice over the clams and serve with crusty bread for dipping. » serves 2 as an entrée, 6 as an appetizer

seafood sauces

Shucked oysters are wonderful topped with a tart mignonette dressing, shrimp cocktail and clams on the half shell call out for spicy cocktail sauce, and I've never met a piece of fried seafood that hasn't benefited from a squirt of lemon and a quick dip in remoulade or tartar sauce.

mignonette sauce

This vinegar-based sauce is a wonderful dressing for shucked oysters.

> ½ cup white or red wine vinegar
> 2 tablespoons finely chopped shallots or sweet onion
> 1 tablespoon coarsely ground white or black pepper
> Salt to taste

Combine the ingredients and chill. » makes about ½ cup

tartar sauce

This mayonnaise-based sauce goes great with fried seafood.

> 1 cup mayonnaise
> 1 tablespoon sweet relish
> 1 tablespoon diced sweet onion
> 2 tablespoons lemon juice
> Salt and pepper to taste

Combine the first four ingredients. Season with salt and pepper, then refrigerate for at least 1 hour before serving. » makes about 1¼ cups

rémoulade sauce

This slightly sweet and slightly savory mayonnaise-based sauce goes perfectly with fried seafood or as a topping for crabcakes.

> ½ cup mayonnaise
> ¼ cup sweet pickle relish
> 2 tablespoons ketchup (optional—although I like a "pink" rémoulade sauce)
> 1 tablespoon capers, chopped
> 1 tablespoon Dijon-style mustard
> 1 tablespoon fresh lemon juice
> ⅛ teaspoon cayenne pepper (optional)

Combine the ingredients and chill. » makes about 1 cup

cocktail sauce

The classic dipping sauce for shrimp cocktail. It's equally good on just-shucked oysters and clams.

> ½ cup ketchup
> 1 to 2 tablespoons horseradish (or more to taste)
> 1 tablespoon fresh lemon juice
> Splash of Tabasco sauce (optional)
> Dash of celery salt (optional)

Combine the ingredients until well mixed. Chill the sauce before serving. » makes about ½ cup

traditional new england clambake

Sure, it takes some effort to throw a traditional clambake, but it's worth it. Recruit some friends to help with the preparations.

materials

Large stones and rocks

Kindling and firewood

Shovel

Coals

Metal rake

4 large rocks or cinder blocks

Large barbecue grate(s)

Seaweed

Large burlap tarp

Saucepan

ingredients (per person)

1 or 2 red Bliss potatoes

1 ear corn

One 1¼-pound lobster

4 ounces linguica sausage (optional)

6 hard-shell clams and/or oysters

Lemon wedges

Butter

TRADITIONAL CLAMBAKE TIPS

» Find out whether you need a permit to build a fire on the beach.

» Start early in the day—it takes hours to prepare the pit and cook the food.

» You'll need a bushel or two of seaweed; if you can't collect it on the beach, order it from your local fishmonger.

» Bring along a fire extinguisher for safety.

---

1. With a shovel, dig a pit 2 feet deep by 3 feet in diameter in the sand and line it with large stones and rocks.

2. Place the kindling and firewood on top of the coals and start a fire, carefully adding logs to fuel it (for tips, see How to Build a Campfire, page 88) Allow the wood to burn for approximately 1 to 2 hours or until the rocks are very hot.

3. When ready, carefully rake off the coals to expose the hot rocks, and position 1 large rock or cinder block in each corner of the pit. Place the barbecue grate on top, and spread a thick layer of seaweed over the grate.

4. Place the potatoes and corn on top of the grate, and cover with a thin layer of seaweed. Next, place the lobster and sausage on top of the grate, and cover with another thin layer of seaweed.

5. Finally, place the clams and/or oysters on top and cover with more seaweed.

6. Drench the burlap tarp in seawater, and place it over the entire clambake to keep in the steam. Throughout the cooking process, keep the tarp wet by pouring seawater over the top when necessary.

7. Allow the food to cook for approximately 1 to 1½ hours, or until the clams open and the lobster turns red.

8. A few minutes before serving, melt the butter in the saucepan.

9. Serve the feast with lemon wedges, melted butter—and cold beer, of course.

HOW TO HAVE A

backyard or indoor clambake

If you're short on time or good weather, bring the clambake indoors.

materials

Lobster pot

Steamer rack

Grill or kitchen stove

Mesh onion bag or
    cheesecloth

String

1 pound seaweed (optional)

Saucepan

ingredients (per person)

1 or 2 red Bliss potatoes

1 ear corn

One 1¼-pound lobster

Hard-shell clams and/or
    oysters

4 ounces linguica sausage
    (optional)

½ cup wine

Lemon wedges

Butter

RESOURCE

Need more than one or two mesh bags for your clambake?

Famous Foods (866-646-4266; www.famousfoods.com)
Look for the Clam Boil Bags, stretchable cheesecloth bags that
measure 18 to 20 inches long. Sold 100 to a pack.

1. Preheat the outdoor grill. (Note: If you are preparing an indoor clambake, disregard this step.)

2. If you are using seaweed, spread half across the bottom of the lobster pot, then place the metal steamer rack on top.

3. Add all the potatoes but one to the pot.

4. Stand the corn upright along the edges of the pot, then place the lobsters in the center. Fill a mesh onion bag or cheesecloth with the clams and oysters, tie the bag closed with the string, and place over the lobsters. Add the sausages, if using. Place the remaining potato on top—this potato will act as a gauge to determine when the food is done. Finally, pour wine or beer over the ingredients and place the remaining seaweed on top, if you are using it.

5. Place the lid on the pot and cook over high heat for approximately 40 to 50 minutes on the grill, or for 30 to 40 minutes on the stove top, or until the potato on the top is tender and the lobsters are bright red.

6. A few minutes before serving, melt the butter in the saucepan.

7. Serve your clambake with lemon wedges and melted butter.

HOW TO catch crabs

My father taught me how to catch crabs when I was just a child, and I've been doing it every summer since. To get started you should contact the local town hall to find out if you need a license or permit to crab in the area. The best place to catch crabs is from a pier, since you'll need to drop your net into at least three feet of water; seasoned crabbers swear that the deeper the pier, the more crabs you'll catch.

If you're planning on crabbing often, consider purchasing a crab net from your local tackle shop; they're relatively inexpensive and can be reused for years. If you just want to while away a few hours one afternoon, you can make a simple net with a mesh bag (like the kind onions come in at the supermarket).

Tie some raw chicken or bacon to the inside of your net, then attach a long piece of nylon rope or fishing line to it. Carefully drop the net into the water; hold the end of the line firmly. After about 5 minutes—or sooner if you feel a tug on the line—slowly pull the bag back up; if you pull too quickly, the crabs may fall off. Hold the net over an empty bucket and carefully release any crabs attached; if they're stubborn, snip the net with scissors. And watch your fingers!

Once caught, crabs must be kept alive until they're cooked. If you are storing your catch while you continue to crab, try to keep your crabs out of direct sunlight. A wet towel or a burlap sack placed over the bucket will shade the crabs and keep them alive. Pouring a bit of water over them periodically will also help, but they should not be left in standing water (crabs left in standing water quickly deplete the water's oxygen and suffocate.) At home, hard-shell crabs will live for two to three days if stored in a cool (50 degrees), moist environment. Do not store crabs in a refrigerator, as it will kill them. Instead, place crabs in a cooler with a layer of ice on the bottom, and fasten a shelf to keep the crabs out of any melted ice water. Keep the lid of the cooler cracked so that fresh air can get in. Before you prepare live crabs, allow them to warm to room temperature. Cold crabs will be lethargic and may appear to be dead, but once they warm up they should become active again. Make sure to discard any dead crabs.

> A bushel of crabs holds about 60 crabs and feeds 10 to 12 people.

PREPARING CRABS

cooking crabs

Blue crabs need to be cooked before you clean them. Simply drop the live crabs in a large pot of boiling salted water and cook for approximately 12 to 15 minutes; they'll turn bright red when done. Drain and allow to cool before cleaning—that is, removing the meat (see below).

To cook Dungeness crabs, boil them for 15 to 18 minutes in salted water; like blue crabs, they'll turn bright red when done. Drain and allow to cool before cleaning. If your recipe calls for uncooked crabmeat, you can clean these before cooking them, but you have to kill the crab first by placing a heavy knife over its belly lengthwise and cutting through by hitting the knife with a mallet.

cleaning crabs

Place a boiled crab on a flat surface, belly side up, and pull off the triangular flap on its underside. Turn the crab over and remove its shell by inserting your thumb between the body and the shell at the rear and pull the shell up. Twist off the claws and legs.

Using a nutcracker, a small hammer, or even a rock, crack open the legs and remove the meat with a small pick. Next, using a spoon or your fingers, scoop out the meat and roe from the inside of the shell.

Finally, pull off the spongy gills and small paddles at the front of the crab and discard. Break the body in half, or use a sharp knife to cut it in half lengthwise and then into quarters. Continue to pick out any meat.

lump crab crabcakes

1 egg

½ cup mayonnaise

2 tablespoons chopped parsley

2 tablespoons chopped chives

1 teaspoon Dijon mustard

1 teaspoon Worcestershire sauce

Salt and pepper to taste

1½ pounds lump crabmeat

¼ cup plain bread crumbs

Lemon slices (optional)

Rémoulade Sauce (page 142) or
 Tartar Sauce (page 142) (optional)

In a large bowl, gently whisk together the egg, mayonnaise, parsley, chives, mustard, and Worcestershire sauce. Season with salt and pepper.

Gently mix in crab and bread crumbs. Cover the mixture and refrigerate for approximately 1 hour.

Preheat the oven to 350°F.

Remove the crab mixture from the refrigerator and, using your hands, shape it into twelve cakes.

Place the crabcakes on a cookie sheet and bake for 8 minutes. Then set the oven to broil and place the crabcakes under the broiler for 2 to 3 minutes, or until golden brown.

When done, remove from the broiler and serve, if you wish, with a squeeze of lemon and a dollop of rémoulade or tartar sauce.

» serves 6

crab salad–stuffed tomatoes

6 large ripe tomatoes

3 cups crabmeat

1½ cups diced celery

Salt and pepper to taste

2 tablespoons fresh lemon juice

5 tablespoons mayonnaise
 (or more to taste)

Lettuce leaves

Cut the top off each tomato, then carefully scoop out the center, leaving a thick shell.

In a mixing bowl, combine the crabmeat, celery, salt, pepper, lemon juice, and mayonnaise. Fill the tomatoes with the crab salad. Place the stuffed tomatoes on a bed of lettuce and serve. » serves 6

variation » Use 3 avocados, cut in half, instead of tomatoes.

baja fish tacos

After a strenuous morning riding the swells, nothing refuels stomach and soul quite like a Baja fish taco. Traditionally, the fish is coated in a beer batter, then fried, but on my last trip to San Diego I had a wonderful grilled fish version, so in the spirit of diversity I've included recipes for both.

grilled fish tacos

1 pound boned, skinned white fish
  (such as mahimahi, halibut, cod)

1 tablespoon olive or vegetable oil

Salt and pepper to taste

6 warm flour or corn tacos

2 cups finely shredded lettuce or
  cabbage

Sour cream, thinned with a bit of water

Salsa or chopped tomatoes

Lime wedges

Cantina Guacamole (optional; page 135)

Rinse the fish and pat dry, then cut into six oblong pieces and lightly coat with oil. Season with a bit of salt and pepper.

Preheat the grill, then grill the fish until flaky, turning once (total time is 3 to 5 minutes).

To assemble the tacos, fill each with one piece of fish, some shredded lettuce or cabbage, a bit of sour cream, salsa, and a squeeze of lime. You can also top with a dollop of guacamole if you'd like. Fold the taco and enjoy. » serves 6

beer-battered fish tacos

1 cup dark beer

1 cup all-purpose flour

½ teaspoon salt

1 pound boned, skinned white fish
  (such as mahimahi, halibut, cod)

Vegetable oil

6 warm corn or flour tacos

2 cups finely shredded lettuce or cabbage

Sour cream or mayonnaise,
  thinned with a bit of water

Salsa or chopped tomatoes

Lime wedges

Cantina Guacamole (optional; page 135)

In a large bowl, whisk the beer, flour, and salt, mixing well. Rinse the fish and pat dry, then cut into six oblong pieces.

In a deep saucepan, heat about 1 inch of vegetable oil to 350° to 360° F. Dip the fish in the batter until completely coated, then gently place into the hot oil, a few pieces at a time. When one side is golden (1 to 2 minutes), turn the fish and continue cooking until done (1 to 2 more minutes). Carefully remove the fish from the oil with a slotted spoon and drain on paper towels. Keep warm.

To assemble the tacos: Fill each with one piece of fish, some shredded lettuce or cabbage, a bit of sour cream, salsa, and a squeeze of lime. You can also top with a dollop of guacamole if you'd like. Fold the taco and enjoy. » serves 6

lobster

If I had to choose between my husband and a two-pound lobster with a side of drawn butter, I would hands down choose my husband. But I sure would be disappointed I didn't get to eat that lobster!

It's hard to imagine that this delicacy was once considered poor man's food and was even used as fish bait, but that was indeed the case in the early 1800s. It wasn't until 1840 that the taste of lobster caught on, thanks to commercial fisheries that began opening in Maine. Soon lobster became a symbol of status, and lobster palaces—where affluent diners showed off their wealth by consuming several lobsters in one sitting—opened in cities across America.

preparing lobsters

LOBSTER TIPS

» Live lobsters should be active with their claws held up (not hanging limply) and their tails curled under.

» Female lobsters have a meatier tail. To distinguish between the males and females, turn the lobster over and locate the tiny set of legs at the point where the tail starts; the male lobster legs are thick and stiff while the female legs are soft and delicate.

» When cooking a lobster, test for doneness. Pull at an antenna—if it comes out easily, the lobster is done.

» A 1½-pound lobster yields 1 to 1½ cups of meat; a 2-pound lobster yields 2 to 2½ cups.

» Soft-shell lobsters take less time; reduce the cooking time by 3 minutes.

STEAMING

1. Fill a large lobster pot so that water comes up the sides about 2 inches. Add 2 tablespoons salt and put the pot over the heat.

2. When the water comes to a rolling boil, place the lobsters in the pot one at a time. Cover the pot. Steam a 1- to 1½-pound lobster for approximately 20 minutes.

GRILLING

Before grilling a lobster, you must kill it. Follow the steps below to kill it humanely.

how to kill a live lobster

1. Make sure the claws are secured by rubber bands.

2. Place your lobster on a cutting board and grasp the tail where it joins the body.

3. With your other hand, place the point of a heavy, sharp knife (facing away from you) into the short horizontal groove in the middle of the lobster's head. Quickly cut all the way through, severing the spinal cord. The lobster can now be grilled whole, or, if you prefer, you can split it in half from the head to the tail. After splitting, remove the sac from the lobster's head as well as the veins running through to the lobster's tail, then grill.

grilling a whole lobster

Place the lobster back side down on a hot grill. Once the shell has turned bright red (8 to 10 minutes for a 1½-pound lobster), turn and grill an additional 3 to 5 minutes until done.

grilling a split lobster

Place the lobster cut side down on a hot grill. Grill for 3 to 5 minutes or until the shell turns a bright red. Turn lobster over, baste with melted butter to prevent the meat from drying out, and cook cut side up for an additional 4 to 8 minutes.

BOILING

1. Fill a large lobster pot three-quarters full of salted water (use 1 tablespoon of salt for each quart of water).

2. Place the pot over the heat and bring the water to a rolling boil.

3. Carefully place the lobsters in the pot one at a time, making sure they're completely submerged.

4. Cover the pot and continue to boil.

5. Cook lobsters as follows: 12 to 15 minutes for a 1-pounder; 15 to 20 minutes for a 1½-pounder; 20 to 25 minutes for a 2- to 3-pounder; and 25 to 30 minutes for a 3½- to 5-pounder.

down east lobster roll

A lobster roll from the famous Red's Eats in Wiscasset, Maine, is a thing of glory, but homemade lobster rolls are also hard to beat. My favorite hot dog roll is Freihofer's, an authentic local New England brand, but any split-top roll will do.

8 ounces cooked lobster meat, torn or cut into bite-size pieces

2 tablespoons mayonnaise

Salt and pepper to taste

1 tablespoon butter, at room temperature

2 hot dog rolls

2 to 4 leaves of butter lettuce (Boston)

Combine the lobster and mayonnaise in a medium bowl, then season to taste with salt and pepper.

Butter the outside surfaces of the hot dog rolls. Heat a large skillet over medium-high heat and place the rolls, buttered side down, in the pan; cook until browned slightly (approximately 2 minutes per side). Fill the toasted rolls with the lettuce leaves, then stuff with the lobster. » serves 2

HOW TO EAT A LOBSTER

» Allow your lobster to cool slightly after cooking. Be careful when cracking the shell as hot water may spill out.

» Remove the claws from the body by gently twisting them off. Crack the claws with a nutcracker, a small hammer, or, in a pinch, a rock. With your fingers or a small pick, push the meat from the tip of the claw out the larger end.

» To get to the tail meat, grab the tail with one hand and the back of the lobster with the other hand and twist to separate the two sections. Break the tail flippers from the tail, then using a fork or your finger, push the tail meat out the other end.

» Diehard lobster lovers crack the body apart to find more meat. Try the cavities where the legs meet the body—even the legs themselves. Simply squeeze or suck the meat out, or use a pick to work it out.

» If you're feeling adventurous, you can also eat the tomalley, the green liver, which is considered a delicacy by lobster gourmets. Not everyone likes it, so tread carefully your first time. Female lobsters also may contain eggs, which appear red and hard or black and gooey depending on their stage of development; these are edible if rinsed first.

We are a nation of barbecue junkies. We spend all winter anticipating the seductive aroma that makes our salivary glands perk up and our bellies grumble, longing for the taste of simple meats cooked slowly over wood or coals until they become so achingly tender that they practically melt in your mouth.

No one can say for certain when barbecue as we know it today began—and I'm wise enough to avoid the raging backyard debates over dry rubs versus wet sauces, cooking times, and cooking methods—but it's pretty certain that it evolved as a method of both preserving meats and tenderizing less than perfect cuts. Here in the Northeast, pretty much anything plunked down on a grill qualifies as barbecue. Throughout much of the rest of the country, however, things get a bit more contentious. In the South, barbecue means pork; pulled pork and pork ribs dominate, as does tangy barbecue sauce. Out in Texas, where cattle are aplenty, beef is at the top of the menu, coated first with a flavorful dry rub. The distinctions may seem subtle—unless you put a Texan and a Southerner together in a backyard and ask them to make dinner.

HOW TO light charcoal

Those of us who are used to using gas grills sometimes forget how to start a fire the old-fashioned way. Here's how:

1. Before starting, read any safety instructions that came with your charcoal grill. To build the fire, you will need a large bag of charcoal briquettes and a large can of charcoal lighter fluid. Note: If you're using self-lighting briquettes skip the lighter fluid and simply stack and light.

2. Stack the briquettes in a pyramid shape near the center of the grill. Using ½ cup of lighter fluid for each 2 pounds of charcoal, douse the briquettes evenly. Allow the fluid to soak in for at least 10 minutes, then light the briquettes with a long fireplace match or barbecue lighter.

3. After approximately 30 minutes, the charcoal should be covered with white ash. Using tongs, spread the briquettes out across the bottom of the grill and start cooking.

note » Spraying lighter fluid on lit coals is dangerous. Why not skip the lighter fluid altogether and invest in a metal chimney starter? Pile the coals in the top part of the chimney starter, put newspaper in the bottom, and light the paper. When the coals get red hot, dump them into the grill. Or make life even easier—buy a grill with an electric starter.

BARBECUE: REGION BY REGION

In **eastern North Carolina**, they like their whole hogs coated in a vinegar-based sauce spiked with black pepper and crushed chili flakes.

Head over to **western North Carolina** for "Lexington-style" barbecue—a smaller piece of meat, such as pork shoulder, is used instead of the whole hog, and tomato is added to the sauce.

South Carolina, much like its neighbor to the north, loves slow-cooked pork. Tomato-based sauce is popular, but many parts of the state use a mustard-based sauce.

When in **Texas**, expect to chow down on beef brisket, patted with a dry rub, then cooked low and slow over mesquite wood without a trace of sauce.

Kansas City is famous for both ribs and brisket. If you're a fan of a thick and tangy tomato-based sauce, this is the place for you.

In **Memphis**, the pork barbecue capital of the world, it's a hodge-podge of techniques and flavors. You can find ribs served both wet (with a sweet and tangy tomato-based sauce) or dry (with a spice rub). And, unlike in the rest of the South, they top off their pulled pork sandwiches with a heap of coleslaw.

ADDING WOOD CHIPS AND HERBS

» wood chips: Soak the chips in water for an hour so they don't burn, then put them over the hot coals. Earthy mesquite, spicy hickory, and sweet cherrywood are good choices.

» herbs: Soak and drain dried herbs, such as rosemary, sage, tarragon, thyme, or bay leaves. Then sprinkle on the hot coals just before cooking.

CLEANING YOUR OUTDOOR GRILL

Use a wire brush dipped in warm, soapy water. Dry the grill, then brush with cooking oil to protect the surface and prevent any food from sticking.

making perfect burgers

Chuck is the most flavorful type of beef for hamburgers. Ideally buy it fresh and have it ground. If buying ground, purchase chuck that has a fat content of at least 15 to 22 percent for flavorful and juicy burgers. If you prefer your burgers well done, purchase meat with a higher fat content, which will allow you to cook them more without drying out.

2 pounds beef chuck, ground	toppings (optional)
1 to 1¼ teaspoons salt	Cheese
½ teaspoon ground black pepper	Ketchup
	Relish
6 hamburger buns	Lettuce
	Pickles
	Tomato slices

Place chilled ground beef in a large bowl and break up with your fingers. Sprinkle with salt and pepper and mix well with your hands.

Divide the meat into six equal portions (approximately 5 ounces each), and form patties that measure about ½ to ¾ inch thick.

Light your grill and when the rack is very hot, begin grilling burgers. Cook about 3 to 4 minutes per side, turning only once. Do not press down on the burgers with the spatula during cooking—that will squeeze out the juices and dry out the burgers.

When done, serve immediately with buns and desired toppings.

» serves 6

BURGER COOKING TIMES: for 1-inch-thick patties	
Rare	4–5 minutes per side
Medium	5–6 minutes per side
Well done	6–7 minutes per side

BBQ COMPETITIONS

In case you're looking for a BBQ-vacation destination, these are some of the top annual festivals. Most take place in the fall, so if you're itching to stretch the BBQ season out, you're in luck.

» World Championship Barbecue Cooking Contest
Memphis, Tennessee / May

» Best of the West Nugget Rib Cook-Off
Sparks, Nevada / Late August

» The American Royal Barbecue
Kansas City, Missouri / October

» Big Pig Jig
Vienna, Georgia / October

» International BBQ Cookers Cookoff
Grand Prairie, Texas / October

finger-lickin' barbecue sauce

This is a simple tomato-based barbecue sauce to prepare in a hurry. If you prefer yours spicier, use more chili powder, Tabasco, and garlic. A dash of cumin or cayenne pepper provides even more kick. If you like a sweeter sauce, try adding some honey to the mix.

2 tablespoons butter

1 onion, grated or finely chopped

2 cloves garlic, minced

1 cup water

1 cup ketchup

¼ cup brown sugar

¼ cup vinegar

3 tablespoons Worcestershire sauce

1 tablespoon chili powder

1 teaspoon Tabasco sauce

¼ teaspoon salt

Melt the butter in a saucepan over medium heat. Add the onion and garlic and cook until soft.

Add the water and the remaining ingredients. Stir until well mixed, then cook over medium-low heat for 30 minutes. » makes about 2 cups

melt-in-your-mouth spareribs

I've tried plenty of rib recipes, but this one not only produces consistently moist and juicy ribs, it's also easy to prepare. Try it with my homemade barbecue sauce or your own recipe.

5 pounds spareribs, cut into serving-size pieces

2 to 3 cups barbecue sauce

oven method

Preheat the oven to 350°F.

Place the ribs in a large shallow roasting pan and bake, uncovered, for 45 minutes.

Remove from the oven and drain off the drippings. Spread the barbecue sauce over the ribs, and bake, uncovered, for 1¼ to 1½ hours, turning and basting every 20 minutes, until the ribs are very tender and well browned.

Note: For even more flavorful ribs, drain the drippings after the first baking, coat the ribs with the barbecue sauce, and allow them to marinate for 4 hours. Then bake as directed above.

barbecue method

Preheat the oven to 350°F.

Wrap the ribs in a sheet of double-thickness aluminum foil and bake in the preheated oven for 1½ hours.

Remove the ribs from the oven; unwrap and drain off the drippings.

In a large, shallow roasting pan, marinate the ribs in the barbecue sauce for 1 to 2 hours.

When ready to cook, preheat the grill to medium temperature, then place the ribs on the grill about 4 inches from the coals.

Grill for approximately 20 minutes, basting frequently and turning often. » serves 6

barbecued beer can chicken

This is my favorite way to prepare chicken on the grill. The beer keeps the chicken moist, while the spice rub creates a delicious flavor. Make a second bird to turn into a flavorful chicken salad for lunch.

for the spice rub

    3 tablespoons brown sugar
    1 1/2 tablespoons paprika
    1 1/2 tablespoons salt
    1 1/2 tablespoons ground black pepper
    1 teaspoon garlic powder

    1 whole chicken, 4 to 5 pounds, giblets removed
    2 teaspoons vegetable or olive oil
    1 can (12 ounces) beer

Prepare your grill.

In a small bowl, combine the spice rub ingredients and set aside.

Rinse the chicken with cold water, pat dry with paper towels. Lightly coat the chicken with oil, then season, inside and out, with the spice rub mixture.

Open the beer can and pour out and discard one-quarter of the beer. Carefully place the can on a flat surface, then lower the chicken onto the beer can so the can fits snugly inside the cavity of the bird. Be careful not to spill the beer.

The chicken will need to cook upright, so carefully place it on the grill and balance it on its two legs and the can—like a tripod.

Close the lid to the grill and cook over indirect medium heat until the juices run clear and the internal temperature reaches 180°F in the thickest part of the thigh (approximately 1 1/4 to 1 1/2 hours).

When done, carefully remove the chicken from the grill, being careful not to spill the hot beer. Allow the bird to rest for approximately 10 minutes before lifting it from the can. Discard the remaining beer, carve the chicken, and serve. » serves 3 to 4

low-country pulled pork

This no-fuss recipe for pulled pork—pork cooked long and slow, then shredded and served with barbecue sauce—is a delicious alternative to everyday burgers.

    1 bone-in pork butt or shoulder roast, about 5 pounds
    2 tablespoons sweet paprika
    2 teaspoons garlic powder
    2 teaspoons onion powder
    1 tablespoon dark brown sugar
    2 teaspoons dry mustard
    1 teaspoon dry thyme leaves
    Salt and pepper to taste
    Barbecue sauce (optional)
    Hamburger buns (optional)

Trim the excess fat from the pork, leaving a good amount on for flavoring.

In a small bowl, combine the paprika, garlic powder, onion powder, sugar, mustard, and thyme; then rub the spice mixture over the pork, patting well so it adheres to the surface.

Place the pork in a shallow bowl or large sealable bag and refrigerate for at least 4 hours or overnight.

Preheat the oven to 300°F.

Season the pork with salt and pepper, then place, fat side up, in a shallow roasting pan. Roast for 5 to 6 hours, or until the meat is very tender and the bone pulls out easily.

Remove the roast from the heat; cover with foil, and let rest at least 15 minutes or up to 1 hour.

Using a fork, shred the pork, discarding the bone and any excess fat. If you wish to use barbecue sauce, pour the desired amount over the shredded meat now and reheat.

Serve as is or in hamburger rolls—with more barbecue sauce on the side. » serves 4

HOW TO grill the perfect steak

» Choose a high-quality piece of meat, such as a filet or porterhouse or rib eye. The meat should be bright red and well marbled (with thin streaks of creamy white fat running through it). Keep in mind that a thin steak (1 to 1½ inches) is always easier to cook than a thick one (over 3 inches).

» Let the steak reach room temperature before grilling.

» If necessary, trim any fat from the steak that exceeds ¼ inch thick. To keep your steaks from curling when cooking, cut through the remaining fat with a sharp knife approximately every 1½ inches

» Lightly coat steaks with olive oil and some cracked pepper.

» Preheat the grill until it's hot, then oil the grate. Place the steaks on the grill for about 1 minute, then turn and grill on the other side for another minute.

» Turn the steaks once again and grill for half the remaining cooking time, then turn again and grill until done.

» Let the steaks rest for 2 to 3 minutes before serving to let the juices flow out from the middle. Your steaks should be nice and juicy.

HOW TO TELL WHEN STEAKS ARE DONE

Because cutting steaks to check for doneness allows juices to escape, use this test instead. Press your index finger against the meat and follow the guidelines below:

Rare will feel soft when pressed

Medium will feel firm but yielding when pressed

Well done will feel firm when pressed

chilly night chili

1 pound lean ground beef

1 large onion, chopped

1 green bell pepper, cored, seeded, and chopped

2½ tablespoons chili powder

1 large clove garlic, minced

1 jalapeno pepper, seeded and chopped

One 28-ounce can diced tomatoes

One 8-ounce can tomato sauce

½ teaspoon ground cumin

One 15-ounce can beans, drained and rinsed (feel free to use whatever beans you prefer, such as chili beans, red beans, or kidney beans)

Sour cream for garnish (optional)

Chopped onion for garnish (optional)

Sauté the beef, onion, and green pepper in a large saucepan over medium heat, stirring until the meat is browned and crumbly. Drain off any excess fat.

Stir in the remaining ingredients—except the beans and the garnishes—and bring to a boil. Cover the chili, reduce the heat, and simmer for about 1½ to 2 hours, stirring occasionally. Then stir in the beans and cook until they are heated through.

Top each serving with a spoonful of sour cream and/or some chopped onion, if you are using them. » serves 6

corn

Sweet corn—what would summer be without it? The important thing to remember when buying fresh corn is that its sweet sugars start converting to starches immediately after it's picked. In a perfect world, you'd buy it, cook it, and eat it on the very day it was harvested. For those of us who aren't neighbors with a farmer, head to the market and shop for ears that feel full in the hand and that have lots of pale and slightly sticky silk poking out the top (the more silk, the more kernels of corn). Husks should be nice and green, not brown, and a kernel should produce a milky juice when popped with your fingernail.

If you're not going to cook and eat your corn on the day you purchase it, it's best to store it in the refrigerator with the husks left on—keeping it cool will help slow down the sugar-starch conversion.

3 THINGS *NOT* TO DO WHEN BOILING CORN

» Don't add salt to the cooking water—it will toughen the corn.

» Don't cool off the hot corn by running it under cold water—it will make it soggy.

» Don't overcook corn—you'll lose the sweet flavor and the kernels will toughen.

farmstand corn chowder

Filled with plenty of corn and chunky potatoes, this soup is a meal in itself.

4 tablespoons unsalted butter

2 onions, diced

5 tablespoons flour

6 cups corn kernels (cooked or raw)

2 potatoes, diced (white or red)

3 cups chicken stock

Salt and pepper to taste

4 cups milk and/or cream

Melt the butter in a large stockpot, then sauté the onions over medium heat in the butter until soft (approximately 10 minutes). Add the flour to the pot, and stir continuously until the flour turns golden (approximately 5 minutes).

Add the corn, potatoes, chicken stock, salt, and pepper, and cook for 20 to 25 minutes or until the potatoes are tender. Remove the soup from the heat and puree half the soup in a blender or food processor, or use an immersion blender.

Combine the puree and soup in a stockpot over medium heat, then add the milk. Reduce the heat to low and cook for 5 minutes. Adjust the seasoning and enjoy. » serves about 6

grilled corn in the husk

1 or 2 ears corn per person

Softened butter for brushing

Salt and pepper to taste

Prepare the grill.

Pull the husks carefully from the corn so the husks remain attached to the bottom of the corn ear. Remove the silk and push the husks back around the ears. Soak in cold water for 10 minutes.

When the grill is ready, drain and grill the corn (while in the husks) on a lightly oiled rack, uncovered. After 10 minutes, turn the ears. After another 10 minutes, carefully pull back the husks and continue to grill the corn, turning, until golden brown (approximately 5 minutes).

To eat, brush the corn with butter and season with salt and pepper.

THE HISTORY OF CORN

In various indigenous languages the word for corn—or maize, which the Spanish adapted from the Taino word mahiz—means "our life," "our mother," or "she who sustains us." The Indians taught the new European settlers how to grow it, grind it into cornmeal, and cook with it. Had the colonists not had it to sustain them through their first brutal New England winter—in the form of corn bread, porridge, soup, fried corn cakes, and pudding—they very well might not have survived.

enjoying tomatoes

bruschetta

This summer appetizer is one of the few dishes that everyone—meat eaters, vegetarians, and even fussy eaters—enjoys. It requires just a few ingredients and very little effort to pull it together.

- 1 loaf French or Italian bread, cut into ½-inch-thick slices
- 1 large garlic clove, cut in half
- 8 (1 ¼ pounds) ripe plum tomatoes, seeded and diced
- 2 tablespoons thinly sliced fresh basil leaves
- 2 tablespoons olive oil
- Salt and pepper to taste

Preheat oven to 350° F.

Place the bread slices on a cookie sheet, then toast in the oven for 8 to 10 minutes on each side or until golden and crusty. (You may also grill outdoors, turning with tongs to brown bread on both sides.)

Remove from the oven and allow to cool slightly. When the bread is cool enough to handle, rub the top of each toast slice with cut side of the garlic. Discard the garlic.

In a small bowl, toss together tomatoes, basil, oil, salt, and pepper. To served, spoon approximately 1 tablespoon of the tomato mixture on each of the toast slices. » serves 8 to 10 as an appetizer; makes approximately 24 bruschetta

italian pasta salad

This delicious pasta salad, provided by my friend Marian, is reminiscent of bruschetta. While it's perfect on its own, if you're looking to serve a heartier meal, diced grilled chicken, diced pepperoni, or tuna packed in olive oil are good additions. Finely chopped garlic or black olives add a nice punch as well.

- 12 plum tomatoes, seeded and diced
- 2 cups shredded basil leaves
- 1 pound mozzarella cheese, cut into ½-inch dice
- ¼ cup olive oil (more, if needed)
- Juice of 1 lemon
- 1 pound rigatoni or ziti pasta
- Salt
- Pepper to taste

In a large bowl, combine the tomatoes, basil, mozzarella, olive oil, and lemon juice. Cover and refrigerate for 1 hour. Cook the pasta in salted, boiling water. When the pasta is done, drain in a colander, rinse with cold water, then shake out as much water as possible. Toss the pasta into the tomato mixture, add salt and pepper, then cover and refrigerate for at least 1 hour before serving. » serves 4 to 6

TOMATO GLOSSARY

Beefsteak » The biggest. They hold together well when sliced, making them ideal for sandwiches. They also cook down well for sauces.

Cherry or Grape » Cherry tomatoes are very small, which makes them great for salads. Grape tomatoes have been bred for high sugar as a snacking "fruit."

Heirloom » An old variety that has been maintained either because it has appealing attributes like extra-large size, unusual coloring, excellent taste and texture, or simply for sentimental reasons.

Hybrid » A new variety created by cross-breeding two different types of tomatoes.

Plum » Thick flesh and very little pulp. Good for canning and sauces.

garden gazpacho

Refreshing, low-calorie, low-fat, and easy to make—gazpacho is the perfect meal for a sweltering day. Feel free to play around with the ingredients below. If you find wonderful yellow tomatoes at your farmstand, add them. Orange peppers? Try them. No cilantro? Parsley works just fine.

6 large tomatoes, seeded and diced into ¼-inch cubes (reserve seeds and juices)

1 red onion, diced

¾ English cucumber, peeled and chopped

1 large red bell pepper, cored, seeded, and chopped

1 large yellow bell pepper, cored, seeded, and chopped

¼ cup cilantro, chopped

2 tablespoons red wine vinegar

Juice of 1 lemon

½ tablespoon Tabasco sauce

Salt and pepper to taste

¼ cup olive oil

8 tablespoons balsamic vinegar

STORING TOMATOES

Ideally, ripe tomatoes should be stored in a cool place that is around 55°F. Never refrigerate them; it will destroy their flavor and texture. If you put unripe tomatoes in a brown paper bag and leave them at room temperature for a day or two, they'll ripen. To speed up the process, add an apple to the bag.

In a large bowl, combine all the ingredients, except the oil and balsamic vinegar. Pour half the mixture into a blender or food processor and blend until smooth. Return to the bowl and stir the soup until combined.

Add more salt and pepper if needed. Slowly drizzle in the oil, mixing and tasting as you go.

Refrigerate the gazpacho for at least 1 hour before serving. When ready to serve, ladle the soup into bowls, drizzle with balsamic vinegar, and serve with toasted bread or croutons. » serves 6 to 8

Watermelon is the gift of summer; colorful packaging on the outside, a beautiful present—every sweet, sticky, juicy messy, seed-filled bite of it—inside.

The 2006 edition of *The Guinness Book of World Records* credits Lloyd Bright for having grown the world's largest watermelon, a behemoth that weighed in at 268.8 pounds. I bet that oversized fruit would have really turned heads in Green River, Utah, where the annual Green River Watermelon Days festival has been held for over one hundred years. Across the country, fruit festivals are perennial celebrations; in Luling, Texas, alone, there's the Luling Watermelon Thump, while over in DeLeon, Texas, two fruits are feted at the DeLeon Peach and Melon Festival. While I've not yet attended any of those events, I understand their appeal, since I can't get enough of this juicy fruit during the summer. Carved into a basket, a watermelon becomes a lovely vessel in which to serve a fruit salad; spiked with vodka, it's a superb social lubricant for an outdoor summer party; frozen with sugar and water and lime juice, it becomes a granita, a sophisticated after-dinner treat. Perhaps the best and simplest way to enjoy watermelon is to just bite into a cool, refreshing, impossibly juicy wedge.

watermelon granita

½ **cup water**

⅔ **cup sugar**

6 **cups cubed watermelon**

Juice from 2 limes

Place the sugar and water in a small saucepan and bring to a boil. Boil for 1 minute, then remove from the heat and allow to cool completely.

Remove the seeds from the watermelon and puree chunks in a blender or food processor, using both the juice and the pulp.

Combine the syrup mixture, the lime juice, and the watermelon puree and stir together.

Place the mixture in a shallow container and freeze for 2 to 3 hours, stirring the mixture and fluffing it with a fork every hour.

Serve the granita just before it freezes completely. » serves 6 to 8

> Watermelon is 92 percent water.

deseeding a watermelon

Seedless watermelon is a nice convenience, but if you can't find one at your local farmstand, it's easy to deseed one on your own.

1. Cut a watermelon in half, widthwise, then in quarters, lengthwise.

2. Cut through the flesh of the melon along the seed line with a paring knife. Now, lift off the piece of the melon you just cut.

3. Using a fork, scrape the seeds from the piece you just removed and from the remaining flesh on the rind.

At the risk of sounding too much like my parents . . . when we were kids, a quarter bought us a delicious Good Humor ice cream straight off the truck. It didn't matter where we were; when we heard those familiar jingling bells on the street, we'd race down the hot pavement with money in hand. Heated debates always ensued: I loved Strawberry Shortcake, my brother Michael loved a Toasted Almond bar, while my brother John went for Chocolate Éclair. The only thing we did agree upon was that ice cream sandwiches were always a good choice.

Whether you prefer the simplicity of a Good Humor bar or the decadence of a hot fudge sundae, there's no denying that ice cream is the official dessert of summer. While the exact origin of this refreshing treat is contentious, folklore has it that the French chef to Charles I of England can be credited for its creation. For dessert at a sumptuous state banquet, he concocted an exciting new dish that was icy cold and resembled fresh-fallen snow. The guests were delighted with the dessert, creamier and sweeter than any they had tasted before. Charles was delighted as well and paid the chef 500 pounds a year to keep his recipe for "frozen cream" a secret. Eventually, however, poor Charles fell into disfavor with his people and was beheaded in 1649. Shortly thereafter, the chef went public with his recipe, and the secret of the frozen cream was a secret no more.

homemade ice cream toppings

dulce de leche

Remove the label from an unopened 14-ounce can of condensed milk.

Put the can in a saucepan, then fill the pan with water so that the can is covered. (Remember, the can should not be opened.)

Boil the can for 2 hours, checking periodically to make sure the can is not bulging and that it is still covered with water. If the can is bulging, take it off the heat and allow it to cool, then punch a tiny hole in the top and reboil.

Remove the can from the heat and allow to cool slightly. Then open the can and pour the milk over the ice cream or use as a spread.
» makes 4 servings

note » if you want a thick dulce de leche to smear on toasted breads, boil the condensed milk for 3 hours.

macerated cherries

1 cup water

1 cup sugar

2 teaspoons vanilla extract

2 teaspoons rum

1 cup pitted cherries

In a medium saucepan, combine the water and sugar and bring to a boil.

Remove from the heat and add the vanilla and rum. Add the cherries to the mixture, then refrigerate overnight. To use, spoon over ice cream or cake. » makes 4 servings

July is National Ice Cream Month. We love it so much that we consume a yearly average of 23.2 quarts per person. Cities topping the list are Portland, Oregon; St. Louis; and Seattle.

fruit sauce

The perfect way to use up overripe raspberries, strawberries, or blackberries.

1 cup berries (raspberries, strawberries, or blackberries)

1 or 2 tablespoons sugar to taste

1 tablespoon water

Mash together the berries with the sugar.

Place the berries and sugar in a small saucepan. Add the water and cook over medium heat, stirring continuously. When the mixture begins to bubble, cook and stir 2 minutes more, until slightly thickened.

Allow to cool before spooning over ice cream or cake. » makes 2 servings

hot fudge sauce

4 ounces bittersweet or semisweet chocolate

2 ounces unsweetened chocolate

3 tablespoons unsalted butter

1/3 cup heavy cream

1/3 cup sugar

1/2 cup light corn syrup

1 teaspoon vanilla extract

Place the chocolates and butter in a double boiler over simmering water. Stir to combine until the chocolate mixture is melted.

Place the cream in a medium saucepan over low heat until warm. Add the sugar and corn syrup to the cream, stirring until the sugar dissolves.

Add the cream mixture to the melted chocolate, and continue to heat over simmering water for 10 minutes, stirring constantly. Add the vanilla.

Spoon over ice cream or cake while still hot. » makes 4 servings

chocolate-covered frozen bananas

I make these banana pops for pool parties and they're gone within minutes.

3 bananas

12 ounces semisweet chocolate

materials

Ice cream sticks

Plastic wrap

Waxed paper or a coated paper plate

Peel the bananas and remove any remaining stringy fibers, then cut in half widthwise.

Insert an ice cream stick through the cut end of each half, cover each banana in plastic wrap and place in freezer until frozen (approximately 3 hours).

Melt the chocolate either on a stove top in a double boiler, or in a microwave. Remove the bananas from the freezer and use a rubber spatula or butter knife to coat the bananas evenly with the chocolate.

Place the pops on waxed paper and freeze until ready to serve. » serves 6

tip » Try running your ice cream scoop under warm water for a few seconds for an easier scooping experience. Or invest in an ice cream scoop that has a defrosting liquid sealed inside the handle.

ice cream sandwiches

2 ¼ cups flour

⅔ cup unsweetened cocoa powder, sifted

½ teaspoon baking soda

½ teaspoon salt

12 tablespoons (1 ½ sticks) unsalted butter, at room temperature

¼ cup solid vegetable shortening

1 ⅓ cups sugar

1 egg

1 tablespoon vanilla extract

1 quart ice cream or gelato of any flavor, softened in the refrigerator for 30 minutes

Position a rack in the center of the oven. Set the oven at 350°F. Have on hand a 4-inch plain round cutter.

In a medium bowl, whisk the flour, cocoa powder, baking soda, and salt; set aside.

In an electric mixer, combine the butter and shortening. Beat at medium speed for 1 minute or until creamy. Add the sugar and continue beating for 2 minutes or until light and smooth.

Beat in the egg, then the vanilla. Remove the bowl from the stand. With a rubber spatula, stir in the flour mixture just until moistened.

Sprinkle a few drops of water on your work surface. Lay a large sheet of waxed paper on it (the water will help the paper stay in place). Divide the dough in half. Place half on the waxed paper, cover with a second sheet of waxed paper, and roll into a rectangle about ¼ inch thick. Slide a large baking sheet under the bottom piece of waxed paper. Refrigerate for 15 minutes.

Repeat with two more sheets of waxed paper and the other half of the dough; chill.

Slip the chilled sheets of dough off the baking sheets and onto your work surface. Line both baking sheets with parchment paper. Return them to the refrigerator.

Cut the dough into 24 rounds. Remove the excess dough. Use a metal spatula to transfer the rounds to the baking sheets. Use a fork to prick each cookie several times, creating a decorative pattern across the top, if you like.

Return one of the sheets to the refrigerator. Bake the other sheet for 13 to 15 minutes or until the cookies are dry to the touch. Cool on the sheet for 3 minutes, then transfer the cookies to a wire rack to cool. Bake the other sheet in the same way. Cool cookies completely.

Spread 12 cookies with about ⅓ cup ice cream, using an offset spatula or a small rubber spatula. Top each with a second cookie. Place them on the largest baking sheet that will fit in your freezer and freeze for 2 hours. Wrap each sandwich in plastic wrap and store in the freezer for up to 2 weeks. » makes 12 sandwiches for kids

Although I don't have children of my own, my nine nieces

and nephews are a constant reminder to me that kids love, above all else, having fun. Before they became too old, and too cool, for such things, I would make up zany games for them to play, wacky crafts to occupy an afternoon. I like to think that I get that trait from my mom; she was always finding everyday items from around the house and turning them into fun things to keep us busy (and out of her hair). For instance, I can still remember the first tin can stilts that she made for me; I had never seen tin can stilts before, so I was very excited at the prospect of being a half a foot taller! One year, she removed the strings from a set of old badminton racquets, sewed on mesh fabric, and turned them into butterfly nets. My brothers and I would set out in search of monarchs, capturing them long enough to carefully examine their frail beauty before setting them free.

You see, keeping kids occupied and happy doesn't necessarily have to cost a lot—all it takes is a little ingenuity and imagination. Rainy day? Some colorful fabric dye and a few articles of white clothing can turn a dreary afternoon into a fun fashion design party; or grab some smooth stones from the garden and have your kids paint their own crazy critter paperweights. When the sun shines, keep them active with hopscotch or jump rope games, or host a neighborhood Kid Olympics in the backyard, complete with water-balloon-throwing contests, three-legged races, and tug-of-war. Little Princesses will love making a crown out of sunny dandelions, and for future entrepreneurs, a lemonade stand is a good lesson in supply and demand. This section may be called "for kids," but there are plenty of clever ideas inside for both the young and the young at heart.

TIE-DYED FABRICS

While no one knows exactly who created the technique known as resist-dyeing, it most likely originated in China during the Tang Dynasty (A.D. 618–902), then spread to Japan, where it became known as *shibori*. The Japanese turned the process into an art form by intricately dyeing their silk robes and kimonos. Here in the United States, tie-dye became popular in the 1960s with the flower power, "do your own thing" generation to express their individuality. Today, tie-dye is used to add color to curtains, pillowcases, scarves, and, of course, T-shirts. Try mixing and matching techniques to create interesting effects, and remember that the dye tends to run when washed, so make sure you wash your newly designed items separately.

HOW TO tie-dye

All-cotton white fabric item (T-shirt, curtains, sarong, scarf)

1 or more colors of fabric dye

Rubber gloves (see Note)

Multiple rubber bands

Newspapers or plastic sheeting to protect your work area

Several large plastic buckets or containers for the dye bath

Long-handled spoon to mix the dye bath

Scissors

An old towel

Paper towels

classic marble pattern

This basic dye technique uses multiple dye colors to achieve a marbled pattern across the fabric.

1. Crunch your item into a ball and bind tightly with multiple rubber bands.

2. Dissolve half a bottle of liquid dye, or one package powdered, in 2 gallons of very hot water for each color to be used.

3. Carefully place the item into the dye bath, beginning with the lightest color. (Move toward the darkest colors with each successive dye bath.) Leave in the solution for 5 to 20 minutes, depending on the intensity of color desired. Stir occasionally to ensure even color distribution.

4. Remove the item from the dye bath and thoroughly rinse with cold water. Squeeze out the excess water with an old towel, then cut the rubber bands and rinse until the water runs clear. Gently squeeze out the excess water again.

5. To add additional colors, bundle the item into a new ball. Repeat the above steps for each color.

6. Rinse thoroughly in cold water and hang to dry.

sunburst pattern

This dye technique creates a bull's-eye effect on fabrics. You can create one large sunburst in the center of a T-shirt or multiple smaller ones.

1. If you are making a T-shirt, gather a section from the center and secure tightly at the base with a rubber band. For other items, decide where you would like the sunbursts to be, then secure that spot with a rubber band.

2. Pull further—leaving about ½ to 1 inch of space—and secure with a second rubber band.

3. Working forward, pull the fabric up a few inches further, and secure with a third rubber band.

4. Create two dye baths. Dissolve half a bottle of liquid dye, or one package powdered, in 2 gallons of very hot water for each color to be used.

5. Dip the center section of the T-shirt or fabric right up to the first rubber band. Hold it there for 5 to 20 minutes, stirring gently from time to time. Don't worry if a bit of dye seeps past the rubber band; that will create an interesting look.

6. Remove the fabric from the bath, and rinse the dyed portion thoroughly under cold running water. Don't remove any of the rubber bands just yet.

7. Now hold the fabric by the center section you just dyed, and dip the other side of the fabric into the second color bath right up to the third rubber band. Hold it there for 5 to 20 minutes, stirring gently. Again, don't worry if some of the dye seeps past the rubber band.

8. Remove the items and rinse thoroughly and carefully. Remove the rubber bands, wash in a mild detergent, rinse again, and hang to dry.

"dip-dye" pattern

Dip dyeing creates wavy horizontal bands of color across your fabric—similar to the look of a rocket pop. You can keep the colors completely separate or let the dyes run together at the ties to create new colors.

1. From top to bottom, bind your item into three sections.

2. Create three dye baths with different colors. For each color, dissolve half a bottle of liquid dye, or one package powdered, in 2 gallons of very hot water.

3. Dip the lowest section of the fabric into the dye right up to the rubber band. Hold it there for 5 to 20 minutes, stirring gently from time to time. Don't worry if a bit of dye seeps past the rubber band; that's all part of the tie-dye look.

4. Remove the item from the bath, and rinse the dyed portion thoroughly under cold running water. Don't remove any of the rubber bands just yet.

5. Dip the top part of the fabric into the second dye right up to the rubber band. Hold it there for 5 to 20 minutes, stirring gently from time to time.

6. Remove the fabric from the bath, and rinse the upper dyed portion thoroughly under cold running water. Remember not to remove any of the rubber bands just yet.

7. Now, fold the item in half right at the middle section between the two sets of rubber bands. Dip the fabric into the third dye bath right up to both sets of rubber bands. Hold it there for 5 to 20 minutes, stirring gently from time to time. Remove the shirt from the dye bath and rinse thoroughly. Remove the rubber bands, wash the shirt in a mild detergent, rinse again, and hang to dry.

note » Wear rubber gloves when preparing, using, or rinsing out dye.

SUNBURST

DIP-DYE

MARBLE

scavenger hunt

The rules of a scavenger hunt couldn't be simpler—individuals or teams try to find all the items on a given list. There are two ways to share your findings at the end of the hunt. The traditional way is to collect everything in a bag or pail. As technology has evolved, there's a new method: players use a digital camera to record their finding each item. The big advantage of the modern method is that the list of items can include things that aren't transportable (for instance, a seagull or footprints at the beach; animal tracks or deer in the woods).

Make sure the kids know how important it is to leave nature as is and respect their surroundings.

To help you get started with a list that your kids will enjoy searching for, here are some suggestions:

» If you're at the beach: seagull, seaweed, driftwood, seashells in three different colors, coral, smooth rock

» If you're in the woods: tree bark, a Y-shaped twig, leaf with insect holes, five different shades of green, clover leaf, pinecone

» To really get everyone thinking, try a more open-ended type of hunt. Have players find things that are: prickly, soft, orange, rough, smooth, smaller than a quarter.

HOW TO USE ALL THOSE seashells

Here are some crafts that are great to make with your kids. Be sure that you or another adult handles the more grown-up parts (e.g., using the power drill) and closely supervises others (e.g., using hot wax). All you need are some seashells, a few tools, a little imagination, and a glue gun and you'll be able to transform almost anything, from picture frames and mirrors to planters and candleholders.

beach house wind chimes

> **Heavy twine**
> **Assorted shells, cleaned and dried**
> **Power drill**
> **Several eye hooks**
> **Medium-sized piece of driftwood
> (about 1 to 1½ feet long)**

create strings of seashells

Cut five or six lengths of heavy twine, each about 2 feet long. You'll need about seven to nine shells for each length of twine.

Carefully drill a small hole through the center of each shell. Tie a double knot at the end of one of the pieces of string, and slide a shell over the string until it stops at the knot. Tie another double knot about 3 inches above the shell, and string another shell down to the new knot. Continue adding shells until you're left with about 3 or 4 inches of string at the top. Repeat this process until you have five or six strings of shells.

prepare the driftwood

Screw an eye hook into the center of the top of the piece of driftwood. Turn the driftwood over, and screw an eye hook into the center of the bottom of the wood.

Tie a string of seashells securely to the hook. Insert another eye hook to right of the first string (approximately 1½ to 2 inches away from the eye hook), and tie another strand of seashells to that hook. Insert another eye hook to the left of the first strand of shells. Continue adding strings in a row until complete.

Test the balance by holding the driftwood by a string tied through the eye hook on top; make adjustments as necessary by removing a shell or two from one or more strings. Hang your new seashell wind chimes on your porch or in your garden.

vacation keepsake jar

> **Strong adhesive glue or a glue gun**
> **Seashells**
> **Jar with lid, cleaned and dried**

With your glue or glue gun, secure the shells around the top and sides of the jar lid. You might want to save your most special shell to place at the top. Allow to dry.

ocean treasure magnets

> **Strong adhesive glue or a glue gun**
> **Seashells or beach glass**
> **Small round magnets**
> **Glitter (optional)**

Glue the shells to the backs of the magnets. If you want to add some sparkle, decorate the shells with a touch of glitter. Allow your magnets to dry before using.

seaside welcome sign

> **Small seashells**
> **Piece of weathered wood
> (from an old barn, or a board
> that washed ashore)**
> **Strong adhesive glue**
> **Two eye hooks**
> **Rope, cord, jute, or rawhide**

Decide what you want your sign to say, and spell it out with your shells. Carefully glue the shells to the wood. When dry, screw the eye hooks into the two corners along the top edge. Cut the cord to the desired length, then tie it securely to both hooks. Hang your sign in a protected place.

seashell votive candles

Wrap up a handful for a thoughtful hostess gift.

- Newspaper
- Block of paraffin
- Knife
- Double boiler
- Small pieces of colored wax from leftover candles (add crayons if candles are uncolored, if desired)
- Measuring cup
- Wicks with attached metal base (available at any crafts store, or online at www.candlewic.com or www.cierracandles.com)
- Assorted shells, cleaned and dried

Cover your work area with newspaper.

Break the paraffin into chunks with a knife and place in the top of a double boiler. If you're making colored candles, add bits of wax from old candles or crayons; keep in mind that the final shade will be a shade or two darker when your candle dries. Place the double boiler over medium heat, bringing the water in the bottom to a simmer. When the wax is melted, carefully pour into a measuring cup with a pour spout.

Insert a wick into the center of each shell, and carefully pour the wax in. Allow your candles to cool for at least 30 minutes, then trim the wicks to 1/2 inch.

summer shadow box

Shadow boxes—framed boxes with glass fronts—are a lovely way to display your summer treasures. I have several around the house filled with sharks' teeth, sand dollars, and beach glass; they inevitably spark conversation—especially the sharks' teeth. Remember never to take living organisms, only those that have washed ashore and died.

- Shadow box (from your local frame store)
- Colored paper or cardboard mat
- Seashells, beach glass, sharks' teeth, interesting stones, or dried flowers
- Strong adhesive glue or a glue gun

Measure the inside of the frame, then cut a piece of colored paper or mat to fit.

After you've figured out how you want your treasures to be displayed—in rows, an interesting pattern, or randomly—carefully glue them into place on the paper or mat. Allow to fully dry, then insert into the shadow box frame and display.

preserving sand dollars » Soak your sand dollar in fresh water, changing the water frequently until the water becomes clear. Carefully remove your sand dollar from the water and place in a protected, sunny spot such as on the porch or a windowsill until it dries.

preserving starfish » Soak the starfish overnight in a 70 percent isopropyl alcohol solution. Carefully remove your starfish from the alcohol and place in a protected sunny spot such as on the porch or a windowsill until it dries. To prevent the legs from curling, gently weigh it down with a light book or a small plate.

to add strength to your dried treasures » If you want to add strength to your dried sand dollar or starfish, soak for approximately 2 hours in a mixture of 1/4 cup all-purpose white glue and 4 cups of water. Carefully remove from the mixture, pat with a paper towel, and allow to dry thoroughly.

SNAIL

SCOTCH BONNET

SUNDIAL

SAND DOLLAR

SCALLOP

OLIVE SHELL

car games

Truth be told, long car rides are not very much fun. Add kids to the mix, and it's amazing that families actually make it from Point A to Point B with their sanity intact. To make your next road trip more bearable, here are a few tried-and-true games and activities to pass the time.

i spy

The first player, or spy, silently selects an object visible to everyone in the car (the object can be inside or outside the car), then gives the rest of the players a clue by saying "I spy something—," giving its shape, color, or size; for instance, "I spy something yellow." The other players then ask questions about the object, in a form to which the spy can answer with only "yes" or "no." The first player to guess the object correctly becomes the new spy, and the game continues.

license plate search

See how many different state license plates you can spot on the road. Can you find Kansas ... Tennessee ... Missouri ... Nevada? What about Hawaii?!!

the alphabet game

The first player should choose a letter of the alphabet (e.g., "S") and think of a word that starts with that letter (e.g., "sunshine"). The next player then has to come up with a different word that begins with that letter (e.g., "silk"). The game continues until one player can no longer think of a new word.

guess the number!

The first player should think of a number between a stated range (e.g., 1–50, or 1–100). Players then take turns trying to guess the correct number by asking yes or no questions such as "Is it more than 50?" "Is it an even number?" or "Can this number be divided into three equal parts?" After someone correctly guesses the number, let another player choose a number for the next round.

twenty questions

The first player should think of something that is either an animal, vegetable, or mineral. The other players have a total of twenty tries to guess what it is by asking questions such as "Does it have eyes?" "Is it orange?" or "Does it bark?" Once someone wins, another player thinks of something new, and the game continues.

map quest

Bring along an extra map, then use stickers or highlighters to mark each road you take on your journey.

journey journal

Buy inexpensive journals or notebooks to document your trip. Make notes about places you visit; decorate the pages with stickers, postcards, trinkets from rest stops; try to describe each stop, location, or landmark. You might want to bring along some magazines, so you can cut out and paste pictures into your journal to illustrate what you've seen along the way (e.g., palm trees, beaches, cows, parks). Alternatively, purchase a few disposable cameras to document your adventure; once you get home, glue the photos into the journal.

a to z

The first player finds the letter "A" on road signs or license plates around them. The next person has to find a "B," the next a "C," and so on. The goal of the game is to get to Z.

pool games

marco polo

Marco Polo requires at least three players. The object of the game is to avoid being tagged by "Marco" (the person who is "it").

1. Choose one person to be "it." That person goes to one end of the swimming pool and closes his or her eyes while the other players gather at the opposite end of the pool.

2. The "it" player counts to ten and shouts "Marco!" In response, all the other players shout "Polo!" With eyes still closed, the "it" player shouts "Marco" at regular intervals while walking or swimming toward the other players (who continue to respond "Polo!" and can move about). The goal is for the "it" player to get close enough to one of the other players to tag him or her!

3. Once a player is tagged, that person becomes "it," and the game continues.

penny diving

1. Throw a handful of pennies (or more, depending on the number of players) into the pool. Players then dive in search of the pennies.

2. The player who recovers the most pennies is the winner.

balloon toss

This game requires an even number of players—at least four.

Water balloons
A towel for each team

1. Divide the players into two teams and give each team a towel.

2. Have each team player grab the ends of his or her towel, then carefully place a water balloon in the middle of one of the towels.

3. Teams should toss and catch the water balloon back and forth with the towels.

4. The first team to drop the balloon loses.

sharks!

The swimming-pool version of "Tag, You're It!"

1. Choose one player to be the "shark."

2. All the players get in the pool with the "shark." The goal is for the "shark" to catch (tag) the other players in the water. When a player is tagged he or she either stands or sits on the side of pool.

3. Once all the players are caught, the last player tagged becomes the "shark," and the game begins again.

cannonball contest

1. Divide the players into two groups: one to do cannonballs, the other to act as judges.

2. Have the cannonball group line up behind a diving board or along a side of the pool. The "cannonballers" then take turns jumping in the water, each trying to make the biggest splash! (Important—first make sure the water is deep enough so no one gets injured.)

3. Have the judges rate each cannonball from one to ten. The cannonballer with the highest score is the winner.

slip and slide

Thick plastic sheeting
Garden hose

1. Lay a long sheet of plastic on a flat, grassy lawn. Have some adults or kids hold down the edges every few feet for safety.

2. Spray the garden hose continuously over the plastic. The kids should run one at a time and slide on their feet, bellies, and butts across the plastic. (Remind the kids to use caution and to not run too fast.)

The fastest human can swim at 6 miles per hour. The fastest mammal—the dolphin—can swim up to 35 miles per hour.

icy toes relay race

Kids' wading pool
Ice cubes

1. Decide how long the game should be; usually 1 to 2 minutes is about the right amount of time.

2. Have players sit on the ground around the wading pool with their feet in the water. When players are ready, throw ice cubes into the pool and yell, "Go!"

3. Using only their feet, players must remove the ice cubes from the pool and place them on the ground.

4. The player who gets the most cubes in the designated time is the winner.

underwater race

1. Line players up at one end of the pool. One by one, each player swims as far as he or she can underwater until the individual needs to come up for air.

2. Once a player surfaces to take a breath, he or she sits on the pool deck, alongside the spot where he or she emerged.

3. The player that swims the farthest is the winner.

backyard fun and games

Bring a bit of old-fashioned fun to your own backyard this summer with these classics.

three-legged race

» You'll need several (approximately 24 inches long) pieces of rope. Mark a starting line with chalk or tape and a finish line 20 to 30 feet apart, depending on the age group. Divide the players into pairs. With the rope, tie one of each pair's ankles together. Make sure you tie a right leg to a left leg so that the pair are facing in the same direction. There should be no loose ends that the players might trip on. Have the players line up at the starting line.

» Call out, "Get ready. Get set. Go!" All teams race toward the finish line, making sure the legs remain tied and that all "three" legs are used. The first team that crosses the finish line wins.

wheelbarrow race

» Mark a starting line and a finish line 20 to 30 feet apart, depending on the age group. Have the players choose partners, then have the teams line up at the starting line. Have one team member bend over and place his or her hands on the ground. The other team member should stand behind his or her partner, reach down, and grab the partner's legs, placing each leg on either side of the holder's waist, making sure to hold on tight!

» Call out, "Get ready. Get set. Go!" With one player walking on his or her hands and the other player holding on to that team member's legs (like he or she is pushing a wheelbarrow), the teams should head toward the finish line. The first team who crosses the finish line wins.

egg toss

» Divide the players into pairs and have them stand a few feet apart from each other. Give each pair an egg.

» Blow a whistle or yell "Go!" to start the game. Players with eggs toss them to their teammates, who try to catch them without breaking. After each successful catch, all pairs of players move a step apart for the next toss. If an egg falls and breaks, that pair is out. The last pair standing with their egg intact wins the game.

note » Instead of eggs try using water balloons—clean-up will be much easier.

egg and spoon race

» Mark a starting line and a finish line 20 to 40 feet apart, depending on the age group. Have players line up at the starting line. Give an egg and a spoon to each player. Players should balance an egg on their spoon.

» Call out, "Get ready. Get set. Go!" With the spoon in one hand, players race to the finish line, making certain they don't use their free hand to steady their egg. If someone drops his or her egg, that person is out of the race. The first one who crosses the finish line wins.

tug-of-war

» You'll need a rope about 120 feet long and 2 bandanas or 2 pieces of string. Mark a line on the ground with chalk or tape; this is the center line (if you want to make it more fun for kids, put a wading pool in the center or make a mud pit for the losers to fall into). Mark the rope in the center, then measure 15 feet from that point in each direction and tie the bandanas or the strings to those points.

» Divide the players into two teams and pick the team captains. Have each captain grab the rope between the knotted bandana and the end. Have the rest of the team line up behind her. (Note: Each person should stand on the opposite side of the rope from the person in front of him.) Adjust the players so the bandana or string is over the center line.

» Call out, "Get ready. Get set. Go!" Team members should begin pulling the rope with both hands as hard as they can, trying to pull the other team's marker over the center line. The players tug and tug until one team loses by letting go, by falling over, or when its knotted bandana crosses the center line marked on the ground.

note » If you decide to make knots in the rope for easier gripping, be sure that they are spaced evenly from the center. Never wrap the rope around your waist or wrists.

potato sack race

» Mark a starting line and a finish line 20 to 40 feet apart, depending on the age group, and give each player a burlap sack.

» Have the players line up at the starting line and step into the sacks. People will need to pull the sacks up and hold on tight to the top.

» Blow a whistle or yell "Go!" to start the race. Players should hop toward the finish line, remaining in the burlap sacks at all times. The first person to cross the finish line wins.

HOW TO PLAY hopscotch

Bet you didn't know that hopscotch began in ancient Britain during the early Roman Empire as a military training exercise for soldiers. Grab a stone and four to six players and start hopping.

Chalk (to draw the hopscotch court)

Markers for each player (usually a small, flat rock)

1. Draw the court on the pavement.

2. Give each player a marker. To begin, the opening player tosses a marker onto the first square. The marker must land completely within the square without touching a line or bouncing out. If not, the player forfeits the turn. If the marker is tossed successfully, the player begins hopping through the court. However, he or she must not land in the square with the marker in it.

» Side-by-side squares are jump/straddled (that means you use both feet to land), with the left foot landing in the left square and the right foot in the right square.

» Single squares must be hopped into on one foot. For the first single square, either foot may be used. When landing on subsequent single squares, the player must use alternate feet.

3. Upon reaching the end of the court, the player must turn around and hop back through the court, moving through the squares in reverse order and stopping to pick up the marker on the way back. If the player successfully completes the sequence, they proceed by tossing the marker into square two and continuing.

4. If while hopping through the court in either direction, a player steps on a line, loses his or her balance and falls, or misses a square, the turn ends. The player does not get credit for that sequence and must redo it on the next turn.

5. The first player to successfully complete every numbered square is the winner!

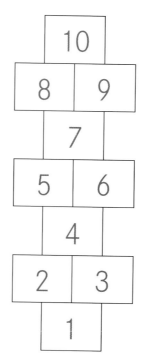

make your own sidewalk chalk

Try splitting this recipe into batches and make each a different color.

- 2 cups water
- 2 cups plaster of paris
- 2 tablespoons tempera paint
- Toilet paper tubes (one side taped closed)
- 1 sheet of cardboard or medium cookie sheet

1. In a large mixing bowl, using a rubber spatula or large wooden spoon, combine the water, plaster of paris, and paint. Allow the mixture to stand for 5 minutes.

2. Place the toilet paper tubes on a sheet of cardboard or a baking sheet, open sides facing up, then carefully pour the chalk mixture into the tubes. If there's any mixture left over, discard it in the trash—not down the drain.

3. When the chalk is just about dry, peel off the tubes and allow your chalk to dry thoroughly (approximately 1 to 1½ hours).

HOW TO whistle on a blade of grass

1. Search your backyard or the woods for a thick piece of grass at least a quarter of an inch wide. Break off the blade of grass close to the ground, so you have a nice long piece to work with.

2. Bring your hands together and position the blade of grass between your thumbs, ensuring that the thickest part of the blade lies taut between the second and third knuckles of your thumbs.

3. Bring the backs of your thumbs facing toward your face. Place the space where the blade of grass lies between your thumbs against your lips. Gently blow through the space, and vary the angle of your hands and intensity of your blowing until you hear a whistle.

4. If at first you don't hear a whistle, adjust the blade of grass so that it lies evenly through the center of the space between your thumbs and try again. If it doesn't work, don't worry—whistling with a blade of grass takes a bit of practice, and you may need to try a few different blades to find the size and shape that works best for you.

HOW TO skip stones

Skipping stones takes a little practice, but once you get the hang of it, you'll want to see how many skips you can get out of one rock.

1. Select a rock that's round, flat, and smooth. It should be less than the size of the palm of your hand.

2. While standing at the edge of a placid lake or pond, hold the rock in your hand horizontally—with the flat side facing down—and your index finger curling around one edge.

3. Throw the rock sidearm—low and parallel to the water's surface—releasing the rock with a snap of the wrist to give it a horizontal spin. Your elbow will be next to your hip as the rock leaves your hand. When done correctly, the rock should skim across the water horizontally. If it doesn't work, try again.

4. Once you get the hang of it, count the number of times the rock skips across the surface of the water. Three is very good. Over eight and you're a stone-skipping expert.

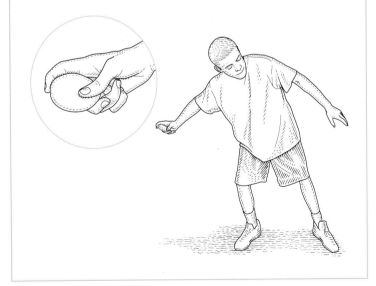

jump rope games

Our days of double Dutch without tripping may be over, but there's always a new generation. For them, here are a few of the old jump rope games and rhymes.

jump the moat

This game needs two jump ropes and at least six players.

1. Two players create the moat by holding the jump ropes low to the ground about 1 foot apart.

2. Jumpers attempt to jump across the moat without landing in the moat or on the ropes. If a jumper misses, they are "out." Once everyone has jumped once, the ropes are moved about 6 inches farther apart, and play resumes.

3. Players continue jumping the ever-widening moat until only one player remains.

4. The player able to jump the farthest wins!

follow the leader

This game requires a long (double) jump rope or 14-foot piece of cotton clothesline and at least four players. By whatever method preferred, one player is designated the leader.

1. Two players begin turning the jump rope. The leader jumps into the rope and performs a specific act or skill, such as hopping on one foot, touching the ground, or spinning around. The leader then exits the rope.

2. Subsequent players attempt to perform the same move as the leader. A player is "out" if he or she fails to jump the rope or correctly mimic the leader's move.

3. The leader must come up with a new move for each round of the game. If the leader fails to jump the rope or perform a new movement, the player is "out."

4. Those who are "out" replace a rope turner and the turner gets to join the jumpers in play.

the dragon's tail

This game requires a long (double) jump rope or 14-foot piece of cotton clothesline and at least three players.

1. The two rope turners lay the rope on the ground, then quickly wiggle it back and forth to create the "dragon's tail." The players then attempt to leap over the dragon's tail without touching it.

2. If the dragon's tail touches a player, that player takes a rope turner's place.

jump rope splash

This game requires a long (double) jump rope or 14-foot piece of cotton clothesline; large plastic tumblers, filled to the brim with water; and at least four players.

1. Two players begin turning the jump rope.

2. The players must jump into the turning rope, holding a cup of water, and complete three consecutive jumps before jumping out.

3. Once all the players have finished jumping, the player with the most water left wins.

jump rope rhymes

Playground rhymes are passed down from generation to generation; once you know one, it's like riding a bike—you never forget. Here are a few of the classics.

miss mary mack

Miss Mary Mack, Mack, Mack
All dressed in black, black, black,
With silver buttons, buttons, buttons,
All down her back, back, back.
She asked her mother, mother, mother,
For fifteen cents, cents, cents,
To see the elephant, elephant, elephant,
Who jumped the fence, fence, fence.
He jumped so high, high, high,
That he touched the sky, sky, sky,
And never came back, back, back,
Till the Fourth of July-ly-ly.

bo-bo ski

Bo-bo ski watten totten,
Ah-ah, ah-ah boom boom boom
Itty bitty wotten totten
Bo-bo ski watten tatten
Bo-bo ski wotten tatten
Freeze please American cheese
  (stop clapping)
Please don't show your teeth to me.
(Resume clapping and repeat verse with
  additions of different things to hide—lips,
  eyes, nose)

miss susie

Miss Susie had a steamboat
The steamboat had a bell
Miss Susie went to heaven
The steamboat went to
Hello, operator
Please give me number nine
And if you disconnect me,
I'll paddle your
Behind the refrigerator
There was a piece of glass
Miss Susie sat upon it and broke her little
Ask me no more questions
Tell me no more lies
The boys are in the girls' room
Pulling down their
Flies are in the meadow,
The bees are in the park
Miss Susie and her boyfriend
Are kissing in the
D-A-R-K
D-A-R-K
D-A-R-K
[fast] DARK, DARK, DARK
Dark is like a movie
A movie's like a show
A show is like a TV screen
And that is all I know
I know I know my mother
I know I know my pa
I know I know my sister
With the alligator bra!

i had a little puppy

I had a little puppy
His name was Tiny Tim
I put him in the bathtub, to see if he could swim
He drank all the water; he ate a bar of soap
The next thing you know he had a bubble in
  his throat.
In came the doctor (person jumps in)
In came the nurse (person jumps in)
In came the lady with the alligator purse
  (person jumps in).
Out went the doctor (person jumps out)
Out went the nurse (person jumps out)
Out went the lady with the alligator purse
  (person jumps out).

ice cream soda

Ice cream soda,
Lemonade punch,
What's the name,
of your honeybunch?
A, B, C, D, E, F . . .
(The letter you miss on is your sweetheart's
  initial!)

a sailor went to sea

A sailor went to sea, sea, sea.
To see what he could see, see, see.
But all that he could see, see, see,
Was the bottom of the deep blue sea, sea, sea.

OTHER THINGS to make and do

This section is dedicated to my mother, for making me realize that fun doesn't necessarily cost a lot; all it takes is a little ingenuity and imagination, and the smiles (and happy memories) will follow.

homemade play dough

3 cups flour

1½ cups salt

3 tablespoons vegetable oil

1 cup water

A few drops of food coloring

Mix all the ingredients in a big bowl, or separate to make different colored dough.

how to make a dandelion chain

1. Scour the yard or woods for dandelions with long, thick stems.

2. Begin knotting your flowers together by tying the stem of one flower in a double knot around the previous dandelion stem, close to the flower. When you reach a desired length, tie the ends of the chain together to secure.

3. Channel your inner fairy princess.

homemade bubbles

Fun for the kid in all of us, but keep in mind that bubbles can create very slippery floors and may stain some furniture and other household surfaces.

basic bubbles

½ cup water

½ cup dishwashing liquid

1 tablespoon cooking oil

Simply mix ingredients together and use with a bubble blower to create a shower of bubbles.

homemade bubble blowers

If you don't have any leftover bubble blowers, these household items can be used in a pinch:

Wire egg dippers from egg-decorating kits.

A piece of wire, a pipe cleaner, or even part of a wire coat hanger bent into a circle.

Cookie cutters.

tin can stilts

2 large juice cans or coffee cans

Swivel can opener

Triangle can opener

2 yards clothesline or cotton rope

1. With the swivel can opener, remove the tops of the cans, then use the triangle can opener to punch two holes on opposite sides of the bottom of the can. Turn the cans upside down so the open ends are on the floor.

2. Cut two lengths of clothesline or rope, each about a yard long. Poke the ends of the rope into each of the punched holes, tying each into a knot to secure the rope. If necessary, adjust the length of the loops to fit your height.

3. Place your feet on the cans, grab hold of the ropes, and carefully stand up.

4. Practice walking on your new stilts.

how to make rock critter paperweights

Try your hand at turning plain old rocks into bright ladybugs, colorful bumblebees, or any other wild and wacky critter you can think of.

Smooth rocks in various sizes

Acrylic paints and paintbrushes

Optional

Glitter glue

Pipe cleaners

Pom-poms

Scissors

Felt

Strong adhesive glue or a glue gun

1. If you are making a multidimensional critter, arrange two rocks to look like the critter of your choice, then glue them together and allow to fully dry. If you are making a simple rock critter, skip to step 2.

2. Paint your rocks to look like the critter of your choice. Allow the paint to dry fully, then decorate with glitter as desired. Add pipe cleaner legs or pom-pom feet. For antennae, twist a pipe cleaner around the critter's neck and twist the ends into curls.

3. Cut out a small piece of felt and glue it on the bottom of the paperweight to protect the furniture. Your critter is complete.

how to make seashell hair clips

Strong adhesive glue or a glue gun

Small seashells in different shapes and sizes

Plain hair clips

Beads, glitter, or small beach stones (optional)

Glue clusters of small seashells to the face of a hair clip. For added sparkle, you can add some beads, glitter, or colorful stones! Allow hair clips to dry before wearing.

how to hula-hoop

1. Lower the hula hoop to about ankle level and step into it with both feet. Bring it up to the area below your waist and above your hips.

2. Plant your feet firmly on the ground, hip distance apart. Holding your hula hoop with both hands, pull it forward so that one side is resting against your back.

3. Fling the hula hoop to the left so that its inner edge rolls in a circle around your body, then circle your pelvis left, back, right, and forward to keep the hula hoop moving around your waist. Your hips should follow the rotation of the hoop.

4. Keep the hula hoop moving

tin can telephone

Talking causes little vibrations in the air in front of your mouth. When you send those vibrations into the can, they cause the back end to vibrate. This vibration moves along the string and into the other can. When that can vibrates, it creates vibrations in the air once again—and you can hear the other person's voice!

2 small soup cans

Swivel can opener

Electrical tape (if needed)

Hammer and awl (or a nail)

Long piece of string

1. Take two small metal soup cans and remove one end on each with the swivel can opener. If there are any sharp edges along the rim, cover them with electrical tape.

2. With a hammer and awl (or a nail) poke a small hole in the bottom of each can. Now take a long piece of string and thread the string through the hole in each can. Tie a knot in each end so it can't pull back through the hole.

3. Hold one can in your hand and have someone stand across the room holding the other, making sure the string is taut. One of you should hold the can to your ear as the other person talks. You'll be surprised at how well you can hear them.

Roller coasters, bumper cars, the Tilt-a-Whirl, the haunted house—there's not an amusement park ride out there that I don't love. During our summer vacations on the Jersey shore, my brothers and I could barely contain our excitement as we sat in the backseat of my parents' old Chevy; the ten-minute ride from our bungalow to the boardwalk seemed like an eternity to us. Once there, we'd ride the bumper cars and the roller coaster, have our palms read, and play skeet ball. If we were lucky enough to be there on a Wednesday night, we'd be treated to the weekly fireworks show that lit up the beach below. But for me, the highlight of our visits was a ride on the giant Ferris wheel. I'd hang on for my life as I was lifted above the clamor of the boardwalk, then gather my nerve and look down to see if I could spot my parents, and all the while I was so afraid to let go of the bar that I didn't dare wave down to them.

The roots of amusement parks can be traced back to medieval Europe, where "pleasure gardens" featured live entertainment, dancing, and games. In America, the amusement park concept caught on in the late 1800s, when they were generally built at the end of trolley lines to increase weekend ridership. These simple parks consisted of picnic grounds, dance halls, and a few rides. In 1893, however, they entered their golden age when the Chicago World's Fair introduced both the Midway, with a wide array of concessions and rides, and the iconic Ferris wheel. Four years later the famous Coney Island resort opened in New York and the public was hooked; by 1919 there were more than 1,500 amusement parks throughout the United States. Today, theme parks have replaced many of them, and while I love the excitement of a wild vertical plunge or spiraling around like a corkscrew, I am a purist at heart: in my book nothing beats a heart-pounding ride on a wooden roller coaster or an old-fashioned Ferris wheel.

amusement parks

8 of North America's best

1 ASTROLAND
coney island, new york

Opened in 1927, the Coney Island Cyclone is the most famous, most copied ride in the world. Charles Lindbergh has been quoted as saying that a ride on the Cyclone was more thrilling than his historic first solo flight across the Atlantic Ocean. Hungry? Grab an all-beef frank at Nathan's Original, a landmark on Coney Island since 1916.

2 PLAYLAND
rye, new york

Built in 1928, Rye Playland was America's first totally planned amusement park and was the prototype for today's theme parks. If you decide to ride the Dragon Coaster, one of the few remaining wooden roller coasters in the United States, prepare yourself to be hurled across 3400 feet of track and plunged 128 feet into the mouth of a fire-breathing dragon. There's also an ice skating rink, a miniature golf course, a pool, and a beach. You can even take old-fashioned pedal boats out on Long Island Sound.

3 SANTA CRUZ BEACH BOARDWALK
santa cruz, california

At California's oldest amusement park, adrenaline junkies can get their fix on a Giant Dipper roller coaster, built in 1924. For those who want to take a walk down memory lane, head to the Looff carousel. Built in 1911, it features one of the few remaining brass ring dispensers in the world, although these days the rings are made of steel.

4 SEASIDE HEIGHTS BOARDWALK
seaside heights, new jersey

Overlooking the Atlantic Ocean, this is the boardwalk from my childhood trips to the Jersey shore. Make sure to ride the giant Ferris wheel that will carry you 160 feet above the crowd. It's the perfect place to watch the fireworks show that takes place every Wednesday night in the summer months.

5 BELMONT PARK
san diego, california

Steps away from Mission Beach, Belmont Park is home to another Giant Dipper roller coaster, one of two oceanfront roller coasters still operating on the West Coast. If you're feeling especially nostalgic, take a ride on the Tilt-a-Whirl, or practice your driving skills on the bumper cars.

6 CEDAR POINT
Sandusky, Ohio

Opened in 1870, Cedar Point is the second-oldest amusement park in North America. Located on a peninsula jutting into Lake Erie, it is also the largest amusement park in the world. It's home to 16 roller coasters, including the Top Thrill Dragster, which travels up 420 feet at 120 miles per hour. A true vacation spot, Cedar Point has four hotels, two campgrounds, a marina, and a water park, making it the perfect choice for thrill-seeking families.

7 KNOEBELS
Elysburg, Pennsylvania

Family-owned and -operated since 1926, Knoebels is a woodsy park featuring two wooden roller coasters, a 1913 carousel, free entertainment, and more than 50 other classic amusements. With camping and a nostalgic atmosphere, this is the park to visit if you're seeking relaxation and rides at a great price.

8 CENTREVILLE AMUSEMENT PARK
Centre Island, Ontario, Canada

Located in the picturesque Toronto Islands—just a quick ferry ride across the harbor from Toronto—Centreville offers 600 acres of parkland with over 30 rides, including an antique windmill Ferris wheel. The Toronto Islands are the perfect place to bike, boat, and picnic, so be sure to enjoy those amusements too. There's even a boardwalk perfect for a scenic stroll.

HOW TO set up a lemonade stand

Lemonade stands are a summer tradition because few people can resist a cold glass of lemonade on a hot day—or the sweet, imploring smiles of the kids manning the stand.

» First, scout for a good spot to set up your stand. If you get a lot of people walking or driving by your house, the foot of your driveway is a good bet. If not, consider going into business with a friend who lives in a better location. Next, determine when the busiest times of day or the weekend are—that is when you should set up your stand.

» Make a large sign to advertise your lemonade, and the price per cup. Price your lemonade to cover all of your costs—such as the expense of the lemons, sugar, cups, ice, a garbage bag, and paper towels— then add in a profit margin for your time. (For example, if your costs add up to $10, and you think you can sell thirty cups of lemonade, price each cup at 50¢, which will bring in $15 total, yielding a $5 profit. And if you sell forty cups instead, you'll have a $10 profit—a 100 percent return on investment!)

» Once you've made the lemonade, head out to your stand with plenty of plastic cups, a cooler filled with ice, a garbage bag to collect used cups, paper towels for spills, and a bag of quarters, dimes, and nickels to make change. If you think you're going to be very busy, keep a backup supply of lemonade in the refrigerator.

» If you are feeling especially entrepreneurial, consider selling cookies as well.

» Don't forget to put on sunscreen before heading outside.

how to fix or cure
just about everything

Cuts, scrapes, bumps, and bruises are a part of life, even more so in the summer months when we're outdoors and active. I keep all of our first-aid supplies, plus emergency numbers and first-aid manuals, in a basket in the bathroom closet so we don't have to go rummaging through drawers and cabinets when we need them. I also pack a few first-aid essentials in a zip-seal bag for road trips and getaways. For those of you who are away from home, or without a first-aid manual, this chapter is a practical guide to helping cure, or at least ease the pain of, common summer ailments.

HOW TO remove mold and mildew

Humid climates breed mold and mildew, which makes your bathroom their favorite place to set up camp. Before you invest in a new shower curtain, try these simple remedies for keeping your bathroom mildew-free.

turn on the lights

Mildew doesn't grow in well-lit areas, so leave the lights on an extra fifteen minutes before and after showering to prevent growth.

keep it clean

Mildew grows on shower walls and doors by feeding on body oils and soap scum trapped in grout, curtains, and tiles. Try this simple recipe:

Fill an empty spray bottle with ½ cup bleach and 2 cups water.

Cover any areas that you don't want to bleach with newspaper or plastic, then spray the affected areas with the bleach solution.

If mold and mildew aren't gone in approximately 15 minutes, reapply.

hang it up

Hang towels, clothing, and anything that can collect moisture on hooks.

après shower

» Turn on the bathroom fan or open a bathroom window to help circulate the air.

» Wipe down the shower and bath area after bathing to remove moisture.

» After each shower, spray shower walls, tiles, curtains, and doors with vinegar.

GET MORE SHOWER POWER

If mineral deposits have clogged up your showerhead, remove it and soak it in vinegar. If necessary, use a scrubbing brush to loosen up caked-on sediments.

removing summer stains

When there's no dry cleaner close by, this handy guide is the next best thing. If you're uncertain about fine fabrics, test on an inconspicuous area first.

alcoholic beverages (other than wine)

Rinse stains immediately with cold water. If a stain remains, apply detergent or dishwashing liquid to the spot while still wet, then launder as usual.

Always treat alcohol stains as soon as possible—they can be colorless at first, but quickly turn brown after standing, washing, and ironing.

ballpoint pen ink

Saturate the stain with an alcohol-based hair spray to break up the ink, then blot with a clean cloth and repeat the process until the stain is removed. If a stain remains, apply detergent or dishwashing liquid, then launder as usual.

berries

Rinse the stain immediately with cool water, then launder as usual. If the stain persists, soak the fabric in a solution of a diaper wash/sanitizer containing sodium percarbonate, or (for whites) chlorinated bleach. For stubborn stains on white cottons and linens, try stretching the fabric over a basin, and pouring boiling water over it.

blood

If the bloodstain is still fresh, sponge it with cool salted water (1 tablespoonful salt per cup water), then rinse with clear water. If the stain persists, rub in a small amount of ammonia and detergent or dishwashing liquid and launder in hot water.

For set bloodstains, try using a meat tenderizer (from the spice section of your supermarket), which breaks down the proteins, allowing the stain to be released. Launder as usual.

butter or animal fat

Apply a small amount of grease solvent, such as Goop, and let it dry. Gently sponge the area with warm water mixed with a bit of shampoo, then launder as usual.

If the stain is on upholstery or carpeting, use an absorbent powder, such as cornstarch, to absorb the oil, then a carpet/rug shampoo or upholstery cleaner.

candle wax or crayons

Make the wax brittle by rubbing an ice cube over it or placing the fabric in the freezer, then scrape off as much as possible with a dull knife or the edge of a credit card. Place the stained fabric between folded paper towels and press with a warm (not hot) iron. Make sure to replace the paper towels frequently to get maximum absorption and to prevent transferring the stain. Continue as long as the wax is being removed. Sponge any remaining stain with a prewash stain remover and blot with paper towels. Allow to dry, then launder as usual.

In the case of colored wax, there may still be a stain, even after laundering. If this is the case, try sponging the area with mixture of $\frac{1}{2}$ cup denatured alcohol and $\frac{1}{2}$ cup of water. Then launder as usual.

chocolate

With a dull knife, scrape off as much chocolate from the fabric as possible, then rinse with cold water. Apply detergent or dishwashing liquid to the spot and allow to sit for 5 to 10 minutes, then soak in cold water for 10 to 15 minutes, rubbing the stain frequently to loosen it. Repeat if necessary, then launder as usual.

coffee or tea

Rinse the stain with cold water. Apply detergent or dishwashing liquid to the spot and launder as usual. If a stain remains, try soaking stain in Borax and warm water (1 tablespoon Borax per cup of warm water) for 30 minutes, then launder as usual.

egg

Scrape away as much as possible, then immediately sponge the area with lukewarm (not hot) water. Apply detergent or dishwashing liquid and launder as usual. If a stain remains, apply a paste of cream of tartar, crushed aspirin, and water on the stained area and allow it to sit for 20 to 30 minutes. Rinse well in warm water, then launder as usual.

glue (water soluble)

Soak the fabric in cool water to loosen the glue, then launder as usual. For carpeting, scrape off as much glue as possible, then blot with a mixture of 1 teaspoon dishwashing liquid and 1 cup water. Rinse and blot with clear water.

grass

Soak the fabric in cold water for at least 30 minutes, then rinse. Sponge the stain with rubbing alcohol and allow to dry. (Don't use alcohol on silk or wool; these will require dry cleaning. If using on acetate, dilute the alcohol 3 parts water to 1 part alcohol.) Rinse with cool water, then launder as usual.

gum

Make the gum brittle by rubbing an ice cube over it, or placing the fabric in the freezer, then scrape off as much as possible with a dull knife or the edge of a credit card. Place the stained fabric between folded paper towels and press with a warm (not hot) iron. Make sure to replace the paper towels frequently to get maximum absorption and to prevent transferring the stain. Continue as long as gum is being removed. Sponge any remaining stain with a prewash stain remover and blot with paper towels. Allow to dry, then launder as usual.

ketchup

Gently scrape off any excess ketchup. Sponge the stained area with cool water, then allow to soak for approximately 30 minutes in cool water. Apply detergent or dishwashing liquid, then launder as usual.

lipstick or makeup

Treat the dry fabric stain with a spot stain remover, then launder as usual.

mildew

Brush or shake off mildewed area. Apply detergent or dishwashing liquid, then launder in hot water; use bleach if suitable for your fabric. If possible, hang outdoors to dry to allow the sun to bleach the fabric.

milk or ice cream

Sponge with lukewarm water. Apply detergent or dishwashing liquid, then launder as usual.

mud

Allow the mud to dry, then brush or scrape off as much as you can. Treat the dry fabric stain with a spot stain remover, then launder as usual.

mustard

Scrape any excess mustard from the fabric. Allow the stain to dry, then soak in a mixture of 1 quart warm water, $\frac{1}{2}$ teaspoon liquid dishwashing detergent, and 1 tablespoon vinegar for 10 to 15 minutes. Rinse in water as hot as is suitable for the fabric, then launder as usual. If any stain remains, repeat the process.

oil (light oils such as baby oil or cooking oil)

Rub detergent or dishwashing liquid into the spot, leave for 10 to 15 minutes, then launder in hot water. If any of the stain remains, repeat the process.

permanent markers

Follow technique for Ballpoint Pen Ink on page 203.

perspiration

New perspiration stains can be removed by sponging with ammonia, then laundering as usual. Older perspiration stains tend to turn yellow, so try sponging the area with 1 tablespoon vinegar mixed with ½ cup water, then launder as usual. If a stain remains, try using a paste of cream of tartar, crushed aspirin, and water on the stained area and allow to sit for 20 to 30 minutes. Rinse well in warm water, then launder as usual.

silly putty

Scrape off the excess Silly Putty with a spoon or blunt knife, then spray the stain with WD-40 and wipe with a soft cloth. If any stain remains, saturate a cotton ball with rubbing alcohol, blot, and rinse. Launder as usual.

skunk smell

Always use cold water on skunk oils, since hot water causes them to break down and smell up the entire house! If possible, wash the clothing with carbolic soap to remove the skunk oil, or purchase a commercial smell remover such as Skunk-Off. If those are not available, soak the clothing in tomato juice, then vinegar, then launder as usual. If the smell remains, repeat the process.

soft drinks

Sponge immediately with cold water and alcohol, as heat and detergent will set the stain. When the fabric dries, apply a spot stain remover, then launder as usual.

soy sauce

Allow the stain to dry, then mix together 3 parts dishwashing liquid with 1 part denatured alcohol. Soak the stained area in this solution for 10 to 15 minutes. Rinse in water as hot as is suitable for the fabric. Launder as usual. If the stain remains, repeat the process.

tomato stains

Use an enzyme presoak spray. Leave for half an hour, then launder as usual.

urine

Soak in a solution of a diaper wash/sanitizer containing sodium percarbonate, or sponge with a solution of 1 tablespoon ammonia mixed with ½ cup warm water. If the stain remains, try soaking in equal parts vinegar and warm water. Rinse well, then launder as usual.

vomit

Scrape or blot away as much of the stain as possible. Sponge the area with warm water containing a little ammonia, or soak in a diaper wash/sanitizer containing sodium percarbonate. Then launder as usual.

wine

for red wine: Immediately pour club soda or white wine on the stain and blot with a clean, white cloth. Sprinkle the stain with table salt, leave on for 3 to 4 minutes, then rinse with equal parts cold water and ammonia. If the stain is set, try dabbing it with equal parts soap and hydrogen peroxide. Launder as usual.

for white wine: Immediately pour club soda on the affected area and blot with a clean white cloth. Wash in cold water and ammonia. If the stain is set, try dabbing it with equal parts soap and hydrogen peroxide. Launder as usual.

wood sap

Scrape off as much of the sap as possible. Sponge the stain with a mixture of 1 part turpentine and 4 parts dishwashing liquid. Leave on for 20 minutes, then launder in hot water. If the stain remains, repeat the process.

curing what ails you

blisters

I've done lots of hiking, and worn plenty of new shoes, so I know blisters. If your blister is relatively small, simply wash it with disinfectant soap and warm water, and apply a bandage or moleskin until it heals. If it's large and painful, you should remove the liquid in it by lancing it with a sterilized needle. Clean the area with disinfectant soap and warm water. Sterilize the tip of a sewing needle by soaking it for several minutes in a disinfectant solution or isopropyl alcohol, or heat it with a lighter or match until it glows red, then cool. Puncture an area at the base of the blister, making sure to leave the roof intact so it can continue to protect your injury, then gently push any fluid out. Apply a dab of antibiotic ointment and cover the area with an adhesive bandage. Check the wound daily for signs of infection (heat, swelling, pain). If you have any of those signs, or a fever, contact your physician.

cuts

Gently wash the wound and the surrounding area with a warm, soft, soapy washcloth. If it's a small area, use a washcloth or tweezers to remove any dirt or debris that might be lodged in it. Once the bleeding has stopped, wipe the cut with Betadine or hydrogen peroxide, apply a dab of antibiotic ointment, and cover with an adhesive bandage. If the cut is deep or if there is heavy bleeding, see a doctor; you may need stitches.

Note: Tetanus shots last only 5 years. If your wound is very dirty, involves rusty metal, or was caused by an animal bite, visit your doctor for a tetanus booster shot.

splinters

Wash the area using a washcloth, disinfectant soap, and warm water. Gently squeeze the splinter with your fingertips to work it out. If this doesn't work, soak the area in warm water for about 5 minutes to soften the skin. Sterilize a sewing needle, a pair of tweezers, and a small pair of nail clippers by soaking them for several minutes in a disinfectant solution or in isopropyl alcohol. With the tip of the needle, carefully make a small hole in the skin above the splinter. Once the splinter becomes visible, try to gently squeeze it through the hole and grab it with the tweezers. If this doesn't work, use the nail clippers to carefully cut the skin away above the splinter, then try to work it out with the tweezers or needle. Once you've removed it, apply a dab of antibiotic ointment and cover the area with an adhesive bandage. If the splinter remains lodged under the skin, call your doctor.

swimmer's ear

If you think you or a family member has swimmer's ear, try to keep water out of the individual's ears for a few days. Usually, these self-help steps can relieve the symptoms: Mix together equal parts isopropyl alcohol and white vinegar, then tip your head to one side and place a few drops of the mixture into your ear canal with an eyedropper. When you're done, tip your head the other way to let the mixture drain out. Don't use a cotton swab, as that can cause damage to your ear. If you experience discomfort or fever, take a pain reliever such as aspirin, ibuprofen, or acetaminophen. Mild heat may help reduce pain as well—try placing a hot water bottle or a warm heating pad on the ear. If the condition doesn't improve within 24 hours; if the individual experiences swollen neck glands, dizziness, or ringing in the ear; or if the ear begins draining a milky fluid, contact the doctor.

PREVENTING TICK BITES

» Wear light-colored clothing outdoors. It makes spotting a tick easier.

» In wooded or grassy areas, tuck your pants into your socks and keep your shirt tucked in.

» Apply insect repellents directly to your clothing.

» Stay on the trails when hiking.

» Inspect clothes frequently. Wash everything when you get home to kill ticks that might be hiding.

» Inspect your body and those of family members thoroughly after a hike. Check belly buttons, armpits, heads, groin, and behind the knees and ears. If necessary, use a mirror to check your back.

» Inspect children who play outdoors at least once a day. In heavily infested areas, check them every 3 to 4 hours.

» Clear the brush immediately around your house and keep grassy areas well mowed.

» Avoid plantings that may attract deer and other animals.

LYME DISEASE SYMPTOMS

In about 50 percent of Lyme disease cases, a characteristic rash begins to show around the bite area within a few days to a few weeks. The rash generally looks like a bull's-eye with light and dark rings. At about the same time that the rash develops, flulike symptoms may start: headache, sore throat, stiff neck, fever, muscle aches, and fatigue. Some people develop the flulike symptoms without getting a rash. If you have any of these symptoms, consult a doctor immediately.

bee stings

Bee stings are painful, but they're generally pretty easy to treat. However, if you begin to feel light-headed or nauseated, break out in hives, vomit, or experience respiratory problems such as coughing and wheezing, get medical attention immediately. These symptoms may indicate the onset of a potentially dangerous allergic reaction.

Don't use tweezers or your fingers to try to pull the stinger out, because that can actually push more venom into the skin. Instead, scrape away the stinger by using a gentle side-to-side motion with a credit card or your fingernail. A small black dot in the wound means part of the stinger is still present.

Once the stinger is removed, wash the area with disinfectant soap and warm water. If you have meat tenderizer in the house, mix a small amount with water to make a paste, then apply it to the area for 15 to 20 minutes. (Insect bites and stings are made up of protein; meat tenderizer breaks proteins down.) An oral antihistamine can help prevent the reaction from spreading, and an anti-itch cream will stop you from scratching the area. Applying a cold ice pack also lessens the pain and brings down the swelling. As noted above, watch for signs of an allergic reaction, which typically will present symptoms within the first few hours.

> Mosquitoes prefer children to adults, and blonds to brunettes.

mosquito bites

As hard as it may be, try not to scratch. Instead, wash the area with disinfectant soap and warm water, and try one of these self-care tips:

» Make a paste with baking soda and water and spread it on the bite.

» Apply calamine lotion.

» Dab with 1 percent hydrocortisone cream.

» Apply an ice pack to help reduce the swelling.

» Hold the area with the bite under warm running water for 10 seconds.

tick bites

Spending time in the woods or backyard is a fun part of summer, but make sure you check yourself and your family often for tick bites; they cause Lyme disease, which can lead to serious health problems. While not all ticks are infected with the disease, if a deer tick does bite you, and Lyme disease is prevalent in your area, make sure you save the tick in a small jar to be tested, then monitor the bite area for symptoms (see box).

To remove a tick, grasp it close to its head or mouth with tweezers or your fingernails. With a slow, steady motion, pull it straight out; be careful not to leave the head embedded in the skin. Wash the area with disinfectant soap and warm water. If any part of the tick remains under your skin, contact your doctor.

BASIC FIRST-AID KIT

» Adhesive tape and gauze

» Antibacterial soap

» Antibiotic ointment

» Antihistamine

» Betadine or hydrogen peroxide

» Calamine lotion

» Cotton balls

» Eyedropper

» Hydrocortisone cream

» Instant ice pack

» Isopropyl alcohol

» Matches or lighter
  (for sterilizing needles)

» Nail clippers

» Needle

» Pain reliever

» Scissors

» Sterile adhesive bandages
  in assorted sizes

» Thermometer

» Tissues

» Tube of petroleum jelly or other
  lubricant

» Tweezers

» Washcloth

poison ivy and poison oak

Both poison ivy and its close relative poison oak contain an irritating oil—urushiol—in their leaves, berries, and roots. Eighty-five percent of the population is allergic to this oil and will develop an itchy, blistery rash up to 48 hours after contact. The rash itself isn't contagious; poison ivy can spread only by scratching the rash during the first few days and spreading the oil to other parts of the body or to another person who might be allergic.

Since contact with urushiol causes the irritation, you may be able to reduce the severity of your rash by immediately washing everything that might have touched it. Rubbing alcohol, beer, wine, or other beverages containing alcohol help to dissolve the resin. Soap works too, but not as well; if you do use soap, use cool water—hot water can open your pores and let more oils in—and wash the afflicted area several times. Soothe the itching with cool, wet compresses, or add 5 cups of ground oatmeal or baking soda to a cool bath and soak for 15 to 30 minutes. The sooner the blisters dry up, the better; lotions containing calamine, alcohol, zinc acetate, or a paste of baking soda or Epsom salts combined with a bit of water will help dry them up. Leave the rash uncovered; the air helps healing. And never break the blisters. If you're very uncomfortable, an antihistamine should provide some relief. Although symptoms will lessen with time, it takes at least three weeks for the rash to disappear completely.

jellyfish stings

While all jellyfish have stinging tentacles, the reaction to being stung can vary, from a mild and temporary prickling or burning sensation, to a severe allergic reaction.

If you've been stung, immediately rinse the affected area with salt water; fresh water will increase your pain. Soak the wound in vinegar or isopropyl alcohol for approximately 30 to 40 minutes to deactivate any remaining cells, then examine the wound, and if necessary remove any imbedded spines using sterile tweezers. If the area is bleeding, apply direct pressure to the wound, then cover the area with a sterile bandage. To relieve itching, apply hydrocortisone cream two to three times a day, but stop immediately at the first signs of infection—swelling, redness, pus, red lines radiating from the site of the wound, heat at the site of the wound, or fever—and get medical treatment. If you show signs of a severe allergic reaction—symptoms might include changes in heart rate, difficulty breathing, or changes in the level of consciousness—call for immediate medical help as well.

heatstroke

Heatstroke is a serious medical emergency. The human body can usually regulate its temperature through sweating, but if a person spends too much time in the heat without taking in enough fluids, the body's cooling processes can't work properly; it becomes dehydrated, and can no longer cool itself by sweating, causing the body temperature to rise significantly. Warning symptoms include cramping, nausea, vomiting, headache, dizziness, and weakness. Once heatstroke starts, signs include skin that is red and hot to the touch, disorientation or acting out of character, seizures, and a body temperature over 104°F.

If you suspect someone is suffering from heatstroke, try to reduce the body temperature. Move the individual out of direct sunlight into a cool, shaded area. Remove any clothes that might retain heat, such as a jacket, sweater, or hat, then have the person lie flat on his or her back with feet elevated. Wet down and fan the individual, or place ice packs on the head, back of neck, armpits, palms, soles of the feet, and groin. If possible, immerse the person in cool water, and use a thermometer to monitor the temperature; when the body temperature reaches 102°F. or lower, remove him or her from the water. Hydrate with plenty of water or a diluted sports beverage, but only if the individual is conscious enough to hold a cup, and drink on his or her own. If body temperature doesn't normalize quickly, seek medical attention immediately.

upset stomach

An upset stomach, or indigestion, can result from overeating, eating spicy, fatty, or acidic foods, drinking too much alcohol or caffeine, and even some medications. Symptoms may include gas, nausea, heartburn, stomach pain, and cramping. Usually these symptoms pass within a day, but if your condition persists, or gets worse, contact your doctor.

» Avoid foods and drinks that may make things worse: coffee, chocolate, fried foods, and legumes and vegetables such as cauliflower and broccoli.

» Ginger works wonders. Try drinking warm ginger ale or ginger tea, or add a few slices of fresh ginger to a cup of hot water.

» Chew on some fresh fennel.

» Drink warm water with lemon.

» Have a cup of peppermint chamomile tea.

» Add a few sprigs of fresh parsley to a glass of warm water.

» Eat a banana.

» Take a warm bath, or lie down with a hot water bottle or heating pad on your stomach.

food poisoning

The chance of getting food poisoning increases in the summer months, when food may go bad in the heat. Symptoms—including vomiting, diarrhea, fever, and stomach cramps—usually present themselves 3 to 36 hours after ingesting the tainted food or beverage, and can last from 12 hours to several days.

Your body needs to expel the bacteria or virus causing the problem, so avoid using over-the-counter medications to control vomiting or diarrhea, as they may inhibit this process. Dehydration is the primary concern, so try to sip small amounts of clear fluids throughout the day. Sports drinks can help replenish electrolytes, and flat ginger ale is a gentle alternative. If you can't keep fluids down, try sucking on ice chips. Once vomiting has stopped, reintroduce food very slowly. Soda crackers, rice, bananas, and plain toast are good choices to help stop diarrhea. Avoid milk and dairy products; fatty, fried, or high-fiber foods; and caffeine until you are fully recovered.

If you experience severe abdominal pain, or your symptoms last more than 24 hours, contact your doctor.

hangover

The best way to avoid a hangover is not to drink alcohol—you'll be guaranteed to never get one. For those who've had one Mai Tai too many, symptoms include headache, nausea, diarrhea, lack of appetite, shakiness, tiredness, and an overall feeling of being unwell. While there's no certain cure, other than time, these tips will help ease the pain.

» Before bed, take two ibuprofen-based pain relievers with a big glass of water; the more water the better. Don't take acetaminophen—combined with alcohol it can potentially cause liver damage.

» Alcohol causes dehydration, so drink as much water as possible to rehydrate cells. If you can handle it, a glass of fresh fruit juice will help perk you up. Avoid coffee as it may dehydrate you even more.

» Eating protein will make you feel better. Try some eggs and toast, or a juicy burger off the grill.

» Replenish lost vitamins and minerals with a multivitamin.

» Take a hot, strong shower. Focus the spray on the back of your neck to open up constricted blood vessels and loosen tense muscles.

» Try a light workout. Exercise increases oxygen flow and helps rid your body of toxins.

» Nothing beats sleep to help your body recover. Try taking a catnap in the afternoon.

» When all else fails, try "a hair of the dog that bit you." A bloody Mary (page 29; try a Virgin Mary if your stomach just can't handle another cocktail) can ease the misery. Tomato juice is full of antioxidants and vitamins, and the alcohol will temporarily dull the pain.

sunburn

Ultraviolet rays are the culprits. We all know what a mild sunburn feels like: red, tender skin that's warm to the touch. More severe sunburn can cause painful blisters or sun poisoning, with its chills, fever, nausea, or rash. If you suspect you or someone in your family has sun poisoning, call your doctor.

To ease the pain of sunburn, take a cool bath or shower. Gently dry off with a soft towel, then apply 100 percent aloe vera gel or hydrocortisone cream to soothe the affected areas. Aspirin or ibuprofen reduces the pain and inflammation, as do cool compresses. Wear the softest, loosest clothing until the symptoms subside. Allow the blisters to break on their own, then apply an antibacterial ointment.

allergies

Pollen and molds—both active in the summer months—can cause sneezing, congestion, and a runny, itchy nose. Minimize allergies with the following tips.

» It's nice sleeping with the window open and fresh air filling the bedroom, but if you suffer from seasonal allergies, you might want to use air conditioning instead to prevent pollens or molds from drifting into your home.

» Minimize your early morning activities, when pollen counts are the highest. After the dew dries, the pollen counts tend to drop.

» Avoid being outside on windy days when dust and pollen are blown about.

» Avoiding mowing your lawn and raking leaves; mowing stirs up pollens, and dry or wet leaves are breeding grounds for mold.

» Don't hang your sheets or clothing out to line-dry.

» Don't overwater indoor plants—wet soil encourages mold growth.

» Keep your car windows closed when traveling.

creature control

Just like we love exploring in the summer months, insects do as well! Ants, bees, mosquitoes, and flies love visiting patios, picnics, and indoor spaces in search of their next meal. (In the case of mosquitoes, that meal would be you!) Don't let biting, buzzing, or crawling critters ruin your summer fun—fight back with these helpful tips.

> The fly swatter was originally called a Fly Bat.

tips for combating ants

» Ants are attracted to food, so make sure you promptly clean up after meals. Place the trash and recycling bins as far from your home as possible, and close them tightly.

» Remove pools of standing water where ants might drink.

» Ants won't walk though baby powder, so sprinkle wherever ants are crawling. Boric acid powder also works.

» Black pepper and chili powder repel ants, and they won't cross a line of ground cinnamon.

» Prevent ants from climbing up picnic table legs by setting each table leg in a can filled with water.

» Mix 1 tablespoon Dr. Bronner's Peppermint Soap (www.drbronner.com) with 2 cups water in a spray bottle. Spray on plants to both kill and repel ants; the soap kills ants on contact, and the peppermint oils will keep future ants away.

» Pour white vinegar directly into the top of an anthill. The acetic acid will kill the insects.

» Use ant traps inside the house.

> The average life expectancy of an ant is 45 to 60 days.

controlling pesky flies

» Like most pests, flies are attracted to food, so make sure you keep food tightly covered.

» Promptly clean up after meals. Place trash and recycling bins as far from your home as possible, and keep the lids on tight.

» Citrus peel and cloves are great repellents—fill small muslin teabags with dried orange peels and ground cloves and hang throughout your home.

» Flies hate basil—place potted basil plants around the house.

» Inspect window screens to make sure there are no holes that flies can slip through. If there are holes in the screens, head to the hardware store for a patch kit (page 215). Or, if the hole exceeds 3 inches in diameter, replace the entire screen.

» Consider installing screen doors to keep flies out.

» Purchase fly swatters—they really do work.

keeping bees away

» Don't waste your time with citronella candles. While they may be effective on mosquitoes, they do little to repel bees and wasps.

» The smoke from a campfire usually relaxes honeybees, making them less likely to sting.

» Bees hate the smell of fabric softener sheets, such as Bounce, so scatter them around the house or picnic area.

» Bees hate the smell of toilet bowl deodorizers—the kind that hang on the rim of your toilet bowl. Don't remove the wrappers; just open slightly and hang.

» Smear marmalade or jam on tree trunks or spoon into small containers and place a distance away from the picnic area. Bees will head there for a free meal.

» If there is a hummingbird feeder outside, make sure no syrup is leaking.

» Bees are attracted to sweet fragrances, so avoid wearing perfumes outdoors.

» Don't swat; swatting at bees simply aggravates them and can lead to a sting.

> Did you know that only honeybees die after an attack? All other stinging insects can continue stinging you again and again.

combating mosquitoes

» Mosquitoes lay their eggs in standing water, so remove or change standing water after 2 days. Check old tires, buckets, plastic swimming pools, bird baths, flower pots, pet dishes, and gutters.

» Inspect window screens to make sure there are no holes that mosquitoes can slip through.

» Keep doors and windows closed tight.

» Seal or screen the holes in the exterior of your house, such as utility holes or dryer vents.

» Mosquitoes often enter a house by "hanging on" to humans, so check your clothing and skin before you head inside.

> Only female mosquitoes bite. They need the protein from the blood to produce their eggs.

AVOIDING MOSQUITO BITES

» Cover up before you go outside. Wear long pants and a long-sleeved shirt. Tucking your pant legs into your socks and tucking shirts into your pants helps to create mosquito-proof seals. Choose light clothing—mosquitoes are drawn to dark colors.

» Wear a hat.

» Treating clothing with a product containing Permethrin keeps mosquitoes at bay and will last for up to five washings. (Don't spray on your skin.) And check out Ex Officio's excellent line of Buzz Off clothing, which has insect repellent built right in.

» If you are not allergic to it, spray vulnerable areas such as ankles, wrists, neck with a repellent containing 30 percent DEET. For young children, look for a pediatric insect repellent with 6 to 10 percent DEET.

» Wash repellents off with warm, soapy water when you go inside.

HOW TO REPAIR a hole in a window screen

Are bugs finding their way inside your home through worn window screens? Repairing holes or replacing screens is relatively easy and inexpensive.

Scissors

Screwdriver

Needle-nosed pliers (for medium-sized holes)

Utility knife (for large holes)

Screen spline roller (for large holes)

for tiny holes

To repair a tiny hole (one smaller than a pea, or less than ⅜ inch across), begin by washing the screen with a mild dish soap and warm water. Allow to dry for 1 to 2 hours. Then, apply a dab of rubber cement or clear nail polish to the tear and let dry. That's all there is to it!

for medium-sized holes

For holes from ⅜ to 3 inches across, head to your local hardware store to purchase a screen patch, which is sometimes sold as part of a kit. (If you have an old screen with the same weave, you can simply cut a patch out with a pair of scissors.) Make sure to cut the patch at least ½ to 1 inch larger than the hole in all directions, then carefully unravel a few strands from each side. Place the patch over the hole, and using needle-nosed pliers (or your fingers if you're very dexterous), carefully weave the unraveled strands into the screen, bending the ends to secure it in place.

for large holes

If the hole is large (bigger than 3 inches), but the aluminum frame is in good condition, you can simply replace the screen mesh. First measure the size of the frame, and purchase a piece of mesh from your local hardware store that extends a few inches beyond its outer edges. Next, remove the screen from the window, and remove the screen mesh from the frame by pulling out the splines (the gray rubber pieces holding the screen mesh in place in the frame) with a screwdriver; set the splines aside. Place the new mesh on top of the empty frame, positioning it so the grids are square with the frame, and using a screen-spline roller (available at hardware stores), push one of the edges of the mesh into one of the channels of the frame. Use the concave wheel of the spline roller to replace the spline. Moving in a circular pattern, continue pushing the mesh, and replacing the splines in the other three sides. When finished, use a sharp utility knife to trim away the excess mesh, and reinstall the screen.

CARING FOR wicker furniture

The word *wicker* is believed to be derived from the Swedish *wika*, which means "to bend." This ancient craft uses natural materials—rattan, cane, reed, bamboo, or willow—that are bent and woven into furniture or baskets. Quality wicker, if kept in a covered, weather-protected environment, will last a lifetime. However, it needs to be cleaned occasionally, since grime and grit get into the crevices.

painting wicker

Painting wicker is messy business, so it's best to do it outdoors on a sunny day.

- Drop cloth
- Face mask (optional)
- Gloves (optional)
- Primer or deglosser (optional)
- Spray-on latex paint (like Krylon)

If your wicker furniture is covered in worn, chipped paint, scrape it off with a wire brush, then clean as per the instructions that follow. To paint your furniture, place it on a drop cloth far away from your house (or other structures that you want to keep fume- and paint-free). If you're worried about breathing in fumes, consider wearing a face mask and, to keep hands clean, a pair of gloves.

Although it's not necessary, applying a primer or deglosser to the furniture helps give you better coverage, more intense color. After it's applied, allow the furniture to dry completely.

Begin painting the wicker with a slow, even back-and-forth motion. Start on the sides of the item for best results, shaking the can every minute or so. Use gentle sweeping motions to get good coverage without causing drips. Be sure to spray from different angles to ensure all exposed surfaces of the wicker are painted.

The paint should be dry to the touch in 15 minutes, and dry enough for another coat in about 1 hour. If the color is uneven or simply not bright enough, apply a second coat.

Allow your furniture to dry completely before using.

cleaning wicker made from paper or grass

To clean wicker made from twisted paper or grasses, simply wipe with a damp cloth.

cleaning wicker made from bamboo, rattan, or willow

To clean wicker that's made of bamboo, rattan, or willow, use a brush or vacuum to remove as much of the surface dirt as possible. Make a cleaning solution by filling a bucket with warm water and 2 to 3 three teaspoons ammonia; dip a sponge or soft brush in the solution and apply to remove the remaining dirt and residue. If the furniture is very dirty, add a bit of mild detergent to the solution and use an old toothbrush to clean hard to reach spots. Keep the amount of water you use on the furniture to a minimum—too much water can damage it. When done cleaning, allow the wicker to air-dry before using.

To restore and freshen unpainted or natural wicker, simply rub it with linseed oil (available at art supply stores), then gently wipe off the excess with a soft cloth. Allow it to dry for several days before using.

two final recipes

If all goes well, you won't have to spend too much time during the summer attending to sick kids or making repairs to your home or summer rental. Summer should be a time for peace and relaxation, so I want to end the book with some more treats to share with family and loved ones.

bananaberry hurricane smoothie

Frozen bananas make this smoothie thicker, but unfrozen are fine, too. No strawberries? Try blueberries, raspberries, or sliced mango.

> 2 cups vanilla ice cream
>
> 1 cup milk
>
> 1 banana peeled and cut into chunks
>
> ½ cup strawberries

Place all the ingredients into a blender and blend until thick and creamy. » serves 2

classic campfire s'mores

We have the Girl Scouts to thank for this messy treat. The name comes from "Gimme some more."

> 1 large marshmallow
>
> 1 graham cracker, broken in half
>
> 1 to 2 squares of chocolate candy bar

Toast the marshmallow until hot and gooey, then place on half the graham cracker and add the chocolate squares. Top with the remaining half of the graham cracker to make a sandwich. » serves 1

acknowledgments

There are many people I would like to thank for helping get this book from my head to your hands.

First, I want to thank my family (the Miksads, the Koloskys, the Wissners, and the Lasagnas) for their endless support and love, for their honest feedback on the many recipes I foisted upon them, and for being the best family I could ever ask for. Special thanks to my Grams for always keeping me in your prayers; you're in mine as well. And to my friends, who hardly saw or heard from me for nine months, yet still listened to me lament about barbecue sauce recipes when they did.

Second, I would like to thank my wonderful agent, Marly Rusoff, for spending her Fourth of July weekend reading my rough first draft, for buying into the idea, and for finding me a welcoming home at Artisan Books. And to Michael Radulescu for always being a kind voice on the other end of the line.

At Artisan, I would like to thank my publisher, Ann Bramson, for not only believing in the book and making it happen, but for personifying the summer spirit by carrying a bathing suit and towel in the trunk of her car at all times. And to everyone at Artisan who helped on the production of this book, especially Trent Duffy for his tireless attention to detail, and Jan Derevjanik for her lovely design.

Special, special thanks to my editor, Laurie Orseck. I know it's a cliché to say "I couldn't have done it without her," but in this case, it's true.

I also want to extend my thanks to all the photographers who submitted many wonderful images of summer. I received hundreds of submissions, and it was hard to edit them down, so the photographers who are included should all be very proud of their work. One in particular—Tara Shriner, an incredibly talented photographer from California, who captured the majority of the photographs found in this book—deserves a special mention. How we managed to find each other across the country still amazes me (thank you, Craigslist), but I am so happy we did.

Love and kisses to "All the Guyz" for making me pancakes and cocoa in the morning, reminding me that summer is just a state of mind, and for giving me bear hugs when I really needed them.

And to Jerry, for more things than I could ever list.

index

photo credits

The author and publishers wish to thank the following for permission to reprint photographs in this book:

Tara Shriner, Tara Shriner Photography, (www.tarashriner.com)
Pages 1, 2 (top row, right; middle right; bottom row, left), 6 (top left; bottom right), 7 (top left; bottom left), 8, 10 (all), 11 (left row, bottom; middle; right row, bottom), 18, 19 (top right), 22, 24, 26, 31, 36 (both), 37, 38, 40, 42 (top left; top right; bottom left); 46 (top), 47, 52 (both), 58 (top row, middle; bottom row, middle), 59 (all except bottom right), 60 (both), 63 (both), 65, 67, 68, 69, 71, 72, 73, 75, 79 (bottom), 81 (top), 98 (right), 100, 108 (top left; top right; center), 109 (all), 111, 117, 126–27, 133, 138, 141 (both), 143 (all), 147, 153, 155, 161, 163, 164, 165 (all), 167, 170–71, 172, 174–75, 178, 179 (all), 183 (top row, middle), 184, 195, 197, 206, 211 (top left; top right; bottom right), and 214; front cover (top row, far right; bottom row, second from left); back cover (top row, left and right; bottom row, second from left and far right).

Pamela Eberhard, Fabulous Pamela Eberhard Photography (www.pamelaeberhardphotography.com)
Pages 27 (top right) and 81 (bottom).

Philip J. Filia, Philip James Photography (www.philipjamesphoto.com)
Pages 2 (top row, left; bottom row, center), 6 (bottom left), 17, 27 (top left; bottom right), 58 (bottom right), 85, 128, 148, and 200; front cover (middle); back cover (bottom row, second from right).

Getty Images
Ross Anania: Page 58 (bottom left).
Jim Arbogast: Pages 11 (right row, top) and 183 (bottom right).
Janis Christie: Pages 19 (top left; bottom left), 27 (bottom left), 35, and 46 (bottom).
Steve Cole: Page 51.
Donna Day: Page 79 (top).
Dex Image: Page 58 (top left).
Ryan McVay: Page 183 (top right).
Anderson Ross: Pages 108 (bottom right; bottom left) and 183 (bottom left); front cover (top left).
Philip-Karen Smith: Page 98 (left).

Jupiter Images
Pages 12 and 41.

Gerry Kolosky
Page 5 (right).

Benjamin Laing, Benjamin Laing Photography (www.laingphoto.com)
Pages 198–99.

Barbara Miksad
Page 5 (left).

Shutterstock
Pages 2 (bottom row, right), 6 (top right), 7 (top right; bottom right), 15, 19 (bottom right), 20–21, 42 (bottom right), 45, 54–55, 56, 59 (bottom right), 82, 83, 84, 86, 95, 97, 99, 101, 104–5, 106, 110, 120, 137, 183 (top row, left), 202, and 211 (bottom left); front cover (bottom left); back cover (top row, center; bottom left).

Chris Tataryn, Karmative Photography (www.karmative.com)
Page 58 (top right).

Thanks are also due to the Red Inn in Provincetown, Massachusetts, which provided the setting for the photo on page 200.